HONG KONG UNVEILED

A JOURNEY OF DISCOVERY THROUGH THE HIDDEN WORLD OF CHINESE CUSTOMS AND CULTURE

Clare Baillieu & Betty Hung

Hong Kong Unveiled
ISBN 978-988-19002-4-1

Copyright © 2012 Clare Baillieu & Betty Hung
Illustrations by Ming

Published by Blacksmith Books
5th Floor, 24 Hollywood Road, Central, Hong Kong
Tel: (+852) 2877 7899
www.blacksmithbooks.com

CONTENTS

continued...

FOREWORD

When talking with Chinese friends or colleagues, many foreign visitors to Hong Kong will hear them say "We Chinese" do this, or "We Chinese" believe that. It is a constant source of surprise that Chinese people can speak of the habits and beliefs of all their millions of compatriots with such certain knowledge that they are right. But generally they are.

To be "Chinese" is much more than belonging to an ethnic grouping. The thousands of years of cultural development, much of it under the same basic national and organisational structure, have developed an enormous set of understandings and procedures that tend to be a total mystery to the majority of non-Chinese. And nowhere is this more true than in tradition-loving Hong Kong. To be a foreigner in any environment is a challenge. But in Hong Kong it seems even more so, given the feeling that all the local population have already been fully briefed in the club rules.

How often do foreigners try to say something in their faltering Cantonese only to have all the Chinese within earshot burst out laughing? When asked why, the answer is usually that one mispronounced a word to a degree that is not discernible to the Western ear, but gives a totally different and often amusing meaning to the Chinese listener.

The Cantonese love their language, and the proper and effective use of it is something they treasure and admire in others, be they fellow Chinese or foreigners. On the one hand they delight in puns and symbolism, with much clever and witty use being made of words that sound like others. On the other hand, for the same reason there are words that should on no account be used in the wrong situation for fear of causing enormous embarrassment or worse.

But this book is more than just a study of the nuances of language. There is much here about Chinese culture. As a foreigner, one can be sure to be the only person sitting at a banquet table who does not know the link between one of the Four Beauties of Chinese history (and yes, there were exactly four) and the place where a waiter stands to serve the food. Do many of us know that it causes more offence to refuse the auspicious roasted pig that is often served at a celebration than not to turn up at all? And what does one do when given a gift by a Chinese – open it or not open it? You can be sure that there is a right way, and a wrong way to behave.

The authors of this book, the one locally-raised and the other a long-term foreign resident, have brought together an insightful blend of instructions and experiences that will be sure to help new arrivals to this city hit the ground running. But even to this expatriate of close on 30 years residence there is much that is informative and extremely useful. Even after such a long time here it is all too easy to put one's foot in it. But reading this book will certainly minimise the risk.

Robert Nield
Past President, Royal Asiatic Society
Hong Kong

A note from the authors

This book is written from a Hong Kong point of view – mainly because the authors have both lived for many years in the territory. It should not be taken, however, to apply solely to Hong Kong but rather a broader view needs be applied.

China is a vast country containing 56 official ethnic groupings or nationalities. Even so, many of the underlying aspects of the culture and customs that are so peculiarly Chinese are common throughout China, crossing all boundaries of race, colour, and creed.

Hong Kong was divided, but not completely divorced, from mainstream Chinese influence during the years of British colonialism. Many of the customs which fell into disuse in some parts of China were faithfully adhered to in Hong Kong. The Chinese have a great inherent sense of homeland and mother country and this adherence to custom, even in the face of scientific and technological evidence to the contrary, is part and parcel of the oneness of Chinese society.

The inscrutable Chinese is just one way in which Westerners seek to explain this oneness. It is more like shared memory, or inherited memory, than anything else, and is lacking in most Western societies.

There are many people we would like to thank for their help in putting this book together. However, we must respect the request for anonymity of so many who freely offered their knowledge and experience. They know who they are and that this book could not have been written without them. Thank you.

Clare Baillieu & Betty Hung

PART I

COMING TO GRIPS WITH CANTONESE

I

CHINESE LANGUAGES

Mandarin, or Putonghua, is the official spoken language in China. Based on Beijing language, it has been modified and standardized by government committee. Mandarin is taught in schools, used in broadcasts, and is the language of the Central Chinese Government.

There are 13 major language streams in various regions, with each stream having numerous dialects. Some aspects of spoken Chinese are common throughout all the languages.

Spoken Chinese is a monosyllabic, tonal, language. What might sound like a sing-song language is just the unaccustomed ear not understanding that it is hearing tones. Exactly the same sound, uttered in a different tone, can be vastly different in meaning. This is one reason the Chinese often repeat back to the speaker his exact words – to check that the speech has been heard correctly.

Exactly the same sounds uttered in exactly the same tones can also have vastly different meanings depending on the rest of the sentence. Chinese are accustomed to being wrong-footed over misunderstandings of this nature; it has led to a culture of language-based jokes which are very popular.

You do not need to have a good ear, or be able to sing in tune, to speak Chinese. The tonal values are within each person's own range and should not be confused with musical notes. There is no set pitch per word; it is relative, taken as a tone different from that before or after it.

In this book, tones are not indicated as the notations tend to be confusing. Each word is represented by its traditional Chinese character (if one exists) so any confusion may be checked in a dictionary or with a Cantonese speaker. Not all words can be written in traditional Chinese; for some there is no character, or if there once was a character it has been lost.

Written Chinese is another kettle of fish. There is a formal, archaic language and many subsets of written languages, perhaps as many as there are spoken Chinese languages. The formal written language, referred to here as traditional Chinese, is not a representation of any spoken language and follows its own rules of grammar and word order. It does not have its own sound, either, but, depending on the spoken language of the reader, the character is allocated a sound in that language.

Chinese writing is based on characters, not an alphabet, and each individual character represents a single word and must be learned by rote.

There are two sets of characters, simplified and traditional. The Central Government of China encourages the use of simplified characters but traditional Chinese is still used and taught in schools in Hong Kong and Taiwan; it is also the written language of choice of many academics and intellectuals.

The characters represent the same words but a person educated in only one set of characters must use some guesswork in reading the other. Not every character has two sets. Only about 1,000 of the most commonly used words, out of a total of about 10,000 characters, is simplified. Most adults have a vocabulary of about 4,000 characters.

The written representations of spoken languages as subsets offer further complications. They "borrow" characters from the formal language, adding an element to indicate that it is being used for its sound alone and that the meaning has been left behind. These characters are mixed in with characters from the formal written language (traditional or simplified). Only a speaker of Cantonese, for instance, can read written Cantonese, as a Mandarin speaker would not necessarily know the sound of the Cantonese word, nor its meaning. In Cyberspace, the use of these informal regional writing styles has ballooned. As the Chinese learn the different slang and particle usages in other regions, they are amazed and often incorporate these new words and phrases into their own lexicon, thus enriching that dialect or language.

That is not the end of the story of reading Chinese. Once the reader identifies in which language the piece is written, he must have a good knowledge of the spoken language in order to understand it. Cantonese, for instance, is rich in allegory and slang usages abound. The Bank of China Building is known as "the box the Hongkong Bank came in," or it was when it was first built. The reference was to the extra-skeletal façade of the Hongkong Bank building (then a ground breaking architectural feature) and the fact that it looks like a Meccano set which came out of a box (the nearby China Bank building) for a child to erect. Political commentary may have been implied. Not many years later, the same term was applied to the Cheung Kong Building and the Bank of China Building reverted to its formal name.

These usages change quickly in the spoken language and, if reduced to writing at the time, their meanings may be lost to posterity as the language changes.

Additionally just a few words or a set phrase might be used to convey the meaning of an entire cautionary tale or parable. In a few words, therefore, the complex character of a man might be drawn, or a social taboo might be explained. This presumes that the reader has a good knowledge of traditional literature which is the basis for most of the references.

This book does not attempt to teach Chinese language but it does use many Cantonese terms. To better enjoy the book, and perhaps to try out some of the terms, a guide to pronunciation follows.

Over the centuries, many systems of Romanisation have been used, each based on the native language of the scholar concerned. The early Jesuits, for example, used the Spanish of the day to explain sounds if they were from Spain. Other priests and scholars used 16th-century Portuguese or Italian. Travelling around the country, the confusion is most obvious in street signs.

The "x" or "xi" refers to a Portuguese pronunciation and is a soft "ch" or "j" sound; "ts" goes back to old Italian and is a more pronounced "ch" sound, but still softer than the English "ch". Yale Romanisation is a more modern system which relies heavily on a knowledge of phonetics and linguistics – it is thus unwieldy for our purposes here.

As authors we have, both from the point of view of a teacher of her native language and of a student of Cantonese as a foreign language, looked at many of the systems of Romanisation used to teach Cantonese and found them all wanting. We have devised our own system based on modern English pronunciation (not 16th-century Spanish or Portuguese) and hope that readers can follow this more readily.

Some **vowel** sounds have no equivalent in English. The following table gives approximations which should be pronounced in the Oxford English manner. Cantonese will then understand your meaning. One vowel sound cannot be represented by an English word and German is used to explain the sound. The final vowel sound of *"Achtung"* is represented by "uung."

a	as in	ma, far
air		hair
ay		hay
e		heck
ee		see(n)
eeu		s<u>ee</u> then y<u>ew</u>
er		fern
ew		yew, newt
i		sing, ming
o (end)		so
o (mid)		upon
oo		soon
or		sore
ow		how, now
oy		soy
u		gum, gut
uu		Achtung (German)
ye		bye

Consonants take their normal English sounds. The "ng" initial consonant has no English equivalent, it is similar to the ng in singing, but said further back in the mouth. "mm" also has no equivalent in English; it is a long "m" said without opening the mouth.

The wisdom and beauty of Chinese characters – an introduction for foreigners

Some Chinese characters require little explanation. Four that spring to mind are: 一, one; 二, two; 三, three and 十, ten. Ten is a cross which represents the perfect axis.

Many characters are pictorial, a simple line drawing of the item described; many are ideograms, depicting an idea in picture form.

八, eight, illustrating things splitting in eight directions.

人, person, people, depicts a person walking.

大, big, depicts a person stretching out his arms and legs, showing you how big it is.

This is added to an ideogrammatic dot to become 太, too much.

Double that and you get 太太, wife, which literally is too much too much.

No matter how big you think you are, there is always something bigger than you: the sky, 天. This big person with his arms and legs stretched out boastfully has the sky, or heaven, sitting on top of his head.

口→古 & 中

口, a pictogram of a mouth – means mouth, oral, etc., it can also mean target.

When added to ten, it takes on the meaning of the generations passing down a story, it becomes ancient 古.

When an arrow hits the target, 中, you get middle.

中國, China, literally means middle kingdom, because Chinese think they live in the centre of the world.

門, door, the picture is obvious.

問, ask. An ideogram composed of two pictograms! A stranger has come to the door to ask (with his mouth) the way.

月, moon, depicts the shape of the new moon; the two lines indicate light emitted.

閒, have free time. If you are standing at the door, enjoying the moonlight, you must have completed your chores and have free time.

朋, friend. Two moons together? How can this happen? Actually, it is a character that looks very similar: a string of money. Two strings must mean wealth is involved. Friends are important. We all need friends and rich friends must be good!

日, sun. This character is square because modern Chinese writing does not use circles, the line in the centre depicts light emitted, like moon.

明, bright. 日, sun and 月, moon shining together.

早, morning. 十, usually ten, here means a scarecrow. The idea is that when a farmer gets up in the morning, he will see the sun rise just above the field, above the scarecrow!

田, field, the picture is clear.

男, man. The lower part of the character depicts the strength of a man's arm, gained from working in the field (the upper part of the character).

女, woman. She is sitting in front of a weaving loom, making clothing for the family. It would be nice to think of it as a picture of her sitting comfortably on a sofa, legs crossed, arms spread. This would not be very Chinese, though, as they are a people who revere work.

子, child. Depicts a baby wrapped in a blanket, holding out its arms: Hug me, please!

好, good. Depicts the perfect family – one boy and one girl. It also represents the idea of man and woman living in harmony, bringing peace to the world.

2

Everyday Usages

Greeting customs

Cantonese only ever greet people they know, however slightly, by saying *jo sun*, 早晨, good morning. There is no saying for good afternoon, good evening, how are you, etc.

To get around this paucity, a series of seemingly obvious questions has arisen such as:

Are you going to work?, *farn guung a?*, 返工牙?;

Have you eaten yet?, *sek jor farn may a?*, 食咗飯未呀?; or

Where are you going?, *hoy been a?*, 去邊呀?

which do not require a factual response. They are the equivalent of the English "Hello, how are you?" No interference with one's personal life is intended. Most people are not interested in where you are going or whether you have eaten, it is a formulaic politeness.

The questions are asked in either Cantonese or English, depending on the language of the person being greeted. To end a conversation, I'll treat you for tea, *cheng nay yum cha*, 請你飲茶,

is an accepted idiom after a favour has been sought. The tea is not expected.

In general conversation, let's have tea some day, *duk harn yum cha* 得閒飲茶, call me, call *ngor,* call 我, or I'll call you, *deen leum,* 電聯, are common farewell phrases. Again, the tea is not expected, nor the call. In English, this is often translated to "keep in touch" and this gives rise to a lot of confusion. It is not meant to be offensive.

Ha lo, 哈囉, a bastardisation of Hello, is a common greeting between people well known to each other. Similarly, *bye bye,* 拜拜, is the most common valediction.

Greeting strangers has a different set of customs. *Nay ho,* 你好, you well, is a common greeting from supermarket workers to customers, for example. Some restaurant chains train their staff to say Welcome, you bring us glory and light, *fun ting gwong lum,* 歡迎光臨. Generally delivered deadpan, it is insincere and can be quite amusing.

Spelling your name

Cantonese pronunciation of the English alphabet can be quite confusing. When trying to spell your name here is a guide to the letters. Where a letter is just listed by itself, it is pronounced in the normal English way.

A, B, C, D, Yee, Airfoo, Zee, Eggchoo, I, Zay, K, Airlo, M, N, O, P, Keeu, Arlo, Airsee, T, U, Wee, Dub Bee U, Exey, Y, and Eezed.

To spell out a double letter, just say the letter twice. Cantonese are not accustomed to hearing "double l" and use of this idiom often confuses.

English interspersed

Cantonese borrow many English words for daily ease of expression, particularly jargon. This is particularly so in the fields of chemistry and computer technology. There are Chinese terms for most, if not all, of these expressions but in Hong Kong, these subjects are mainly taught in English and the language of the classroom spills over into everyday life.

English is also used for simplification where the Cantonese would be a complex and lengthy sentence. This is not a habit in other Chinese languages such as Mandarin.

Everyday examples are "fit" and "call."

Nay ho fit *wor!* 你好fit喎. You look very fit! The Cantonese would be *nay dee gay yuk ho git sut!* 你啲肌肉好結實, your muscle is firm, or *nay sun tye ho geen hong!* 你身體好健康, you're in good health.

Call *nay*, call 你, I will call you. The Cantonese would be *da deen wa bay nay*, 打電話畀你, hit the electric speak to you.

La and other sentence endings

There are many sentence endings used to express different emotions in Cantonese. Some of these words have other meanings but the majority do not. The habit is carried over into English using a mixture of the two languages.

Lo ar, no 啊, no. I don't want it, *lo ar*! Stop that, *lo ar*!

O kay wor, OK 㖞, so so. The food is *O kay wor*.

O kay la, OK 啦, is it possible? (Will you take) thirty dollars, *O kay la*?

Yair see la, yes 啦, please, please say yes. Will you marry me, *yair see la*?

Sor lee lor, sorry 囉, insincere apology. If that offended you, *sor lee lor*!

Cantonese tend to confuse "n" and "l" when speaking English. It is also common to substitute "l" for "n" in informal Cantonese speech. The formal *nay* (you) becomes *lay*, for instance, in casual speech.

The initial "r" sound in English is foreign to the Cantonese tongue, most people simply cannot pronounce "r" and it comes out as "l".

3

How Good Need Your Chinese Be?

Chinese are delighted to hear a foreigner speak just a few words in their language, particularly if the words are said at the right moment. The following examples are given in Cantonese, but could just as easily be in any other Chinese language.

A timely thank you, *dor jair*, 多謝, good morning, *jo sun*, 早晨, oh no!, *aye ya*, 哎吔, or crazy, *chee seen*, 黐線, will be greatly appreciated.

Many foreigners are disheartened when they try to communicate in Chinese and are answered in English. Generally, it is intended as a kindness to speak the other's language back to him. Chinese tend to be impatient at the best of times and in an effort to be friendly and to deal with your question they will, no matter how poor their English, attempt to answer you in your own language. This is also based on the incorrect assumption that all foreigners speak English.

Foreigners are not expected to be able to speak Chinese. Therefore, if a foreigner speaks Chinese it is such a surprise that the words will be repeated queryingly, to check that the listener has correctly understood the meaning. This habit might seem rude but it is not meant to be and is not confined to foreigners. It happens amongst the Chinese also.

There is one other habit of the Chinese when it comes to speaking their language which can be very off-putting. That is the habit of being told, "I don't speak English" when you have spoken to a local in Chinese. As a foreigner, you are not really expected to be able to speak the local language. Mandarin, perhaps, but not Cantonese or Shanghainese or Fujianese. You are expected to speak English and so that is what the person thinks he has heard – and if he doesn't understand it, he doesn't have to deal with it!

Taxi drivers and some doormen in residential buildings are more likely to take the trouble to speak to foreigners in Chinese. However, the majority of shopkeepers and service providers do not exhibit this sort of patience and a common reaction is to laugh in the face of the Chinese learner. This laughter is not meant unkindly. It is part of the culture of language as a source of amusement because the words remind them of something else, it may be nervous laughter because your words are not quite understood, or it may be plain amazement that your Chinese is so good.

Q: I am speaking Chinese! Why won't they understand? What's wrong? Is my accent so terrible?

A: No, it's just that you don't look Chinese, so you are not expected to speak it!

Chinese, once they discover that a foreigner speaks their language, tend to rattle on at great length in colloquial Chinese. This is frequently beyond the scope of the foreigner's language skills and there seems to be little understanding that people might speak just a bit of Chinese, not enough to have a normal conversation. When they discover this, Chinese tend to revert to English and will no longer use Chinese as a communication tool. It makes the language more difficult to learn!

PART II

TRANSLATIONAL AND CULTURAL CONFUSIONS

4

MISTRANSLATIONS

Yes or no

Words for "yes" and "no" do not exist in any Chinese language. The structure of the language is to repeat the verb or adjective of the question in its positive form for yes, and in its negative form for no.

Is that true? *Hye mm hye a,* 係唔係呀?

Yes, it's true. *Hye a,* 係呀, literally true with a following confirming particle; or

No, it's not true, *mm hye,* 唔係, literally true with a preceding negative particle.

Reflexive questions in English create particular problems for the native Chinese speaker who is generally unsure whether to answer in the affirmative or the negative since the grammar of the two languages is so different.

For example, "you're not coming, are you?" "*nay mm lye duck a hor,* 你唔嚟得呀可?" expects the Chinese answer, "yes, I'm not coming." "*hye ah, ngor mm lye duck* 係呀,我唔嚟得." In English the expected answer is, "no, I'm not."

Singular or plural?

Chinese words are not generally pluralised. The context tells the listener if one or more than one is in question. When speaking English as a second language, the idea that a choice must be made whether to use a noun or verb in its singular or plural form is just too hard. Most people default to the Chinese style and use the singular for all purposes.

Masculine or feminine?

The spoken Chinese for he, she, and it, is the same word. The gender of the pronoun is not differentiated and if it sounds odd to hear "Mr Brown's not here, she went to a meeting" it is just because to a native Chinese speaker the gender of the pronoun is irrelevant.

Just wait

Is a direct translation of *dung ha la*, 等下啦, wait a little please, which is a very polite phrase in Cantonese. The speaker is trying say "I'll be with you in a moment."

It can also mean "I'll take care of it," "I'll handle your case in a moment," "Your problem will be solved momentarily," or "You don't have to worry or do anything else."

As a bald assertion in English, it can easily be taken as sarcastic and quite offensive. There is no such intention and as with many translations the golden rule is give the speaker the benefit of the doubt, Chinese go out of their way to ease life along and if they intended offence you would know about it!

Take your time

A direct translation of *marn marn lye*, 慢慢嚟, there's no rush, do this slowly. Polite in the original Chinese, depending on the circumstances it can be most offensive in English. The speaker may be trying to say that what you are doing is not interfering with him at all; or that if you embark on a particular course of action it will necessitate a large input from you in terms of your time.

> This particular mistranslation was the impetus behind this book. Hung used the phrase to reply to a student who had asked how he could speed up learning Chinese. On being told he should take his time, he was so incensed that he wrote to the university and complained. Baillieu knocked over a pile of books in a second-hand bookshop and apologised to a couple who were trying to get past. When told to take her time, her immediate reaction was "who does that arrogant young pup think he is?"

Thank you and excuse me

Both are *mm goy*, 唔該, in Cantonese. They tend to be confused in translation to English.

Large numbers

The system of counting in China is different from the rest of the world. Numbers are still based on the decimal system but the grouping is different. A unit of 10,000 is a common measurement and any Chinese dealing with foreigners quickly becomes aware that he thinks about numbers differently.

Chinese prefer to avoid any misunderstanding when it comes to figures, so often the basis of business dealings gone wrong. Therefore, to communicate large numbers, figures are reduced to writing and the use of a calculator to display the total is preferred.

In shops, assistants often use a calculator to communicate the price of any and all goods and services. If you wish to suggest a different price, it is quite acceptable to clear the display and put your own numbers on the screen. There is less and less bargaining these days, however, and your offer will not necessarily even be entertained.

Outlook

Generally, when Chinese say "outlook" in English, they mean appearance. This is because the Chinese expression for appearance or façade is "outside look," *ngoy gwoon,* 外觀.

Talkative

If someone is described as talkative in Chinese, it means that he or she is a people person, someone who enjoys good inter-personal relationships. There is no belittling inference as carried in English where "talkative" is used to mean someone who does not know when to keep quiet. Talkative is likely to be taken and meant as a compliment by Chinese.

5

CULTURAL ANOMALIES

Dumb insolence – the 'Mm Jo Mm Chor' mentality

When a shopkeeper or a doctor's receptionist, for instance, is asked a question and responds with a blank stare and complete silence, it tends to fray the temper. This reaction stems from the Cantonese saying *dor jo dor chor, seeu jo seeu chor, mm jo mm chor,* 多做多錯, 少做少錯, 唔做唔錯. Roughly translated this means as the more you do the more mistakes you make, the less you do the fewer mistakes you make; if you do nothing you make no mistakes and this, of course, is not bad.

The *mm chor* of not bad is also used to mean quite good, okay, etc. How is your daughter's new job? *Mm chor*, quite good!

To most Cantonese, silence is infinitely preferable to admitting to not knowing the answer, or giving information which may be wrong (and risk being held responsible for it). Therefore, to simply ignore a question is a way of avoiding responsibility and/ or offering a reply which might turn out to be wrong and thus bring about loss of face.

Imperial time

Old days

Upbringing

Meeting

Responsibility is not lightly taken. Another common way of avoiding responsibility is to refer the questioner to another department (especially in Government offices), or to state, "that's not my responsibility" and resort to silence.

The Chinese smile

A smile from a Cantonese does not necessarily indicate happiness or pleasure, as one might expect from a Western viewpoint. This is also common in Japan, Indonesia, the Philippines, Vietnam, Thailand, and many other Asian countries. It does not extend to northern China where smiles are rare.

A smile is used to soften the blow of bad news. For instance, your boss might smile at you broadly while telling you "you're sacked." You are not being laughed at, you are being consoled.

Smiling is also used to hide embarrassment, often with dumb insolence attached. A smile will be hidden behind by someone who does not want to admit a mistake has been made or that a precious article has been broken.

These smilers are not aware of the enormous offence that their well-intentioned smiles can cause and are surprised and often hurt when told to wipe the smiles off their faces.

Baby talk and word stresses

Voice-overs on television advertisements and personal service providers such as masseuses often use baby talk to adults. This is done in an effort to be more polite and friendly, it is not intended to be patronising.

A Westerner may use a higher pitch to indicate excitement or a rising tone to indicate disbelief. Since Cantonese is a tonal language, these indicators are not used as they may change the meaning of the words. Instead, a word it may be drawn out to an exaggerated length to express excitement or have extra syllables added; to express disbelief, an additional particle is added.

That's right, *hye*.

That's definitely right, *hye*. (with an emphatic nod)

That's right! *Hye luk*! (with a hand gesture)

Tell me that's not right! *Hye mair*!? (with head thrust forward)

Media scaremongering

Any news affecting health and diet is treated as a front-page sensational item. The topic also becomes one for casual conversation and if, say, it is discovered that some food product is polluted or has a slightly higher than standard content of a heavy metal, the result is likely to be that the whole town will eschew jellyfish, for instance.

As a result of scaremongering over dim sum and the oiliness of some types, certain selections are now very hard to come by. *Ho Wong Seen Jook Gewn*, 蠔皇鮮竹卷, fried beancurd roll in oyster sauce, for instance, is now generally served in soup – which sounds healthier but in fact the roll is prepared exactly the same way, it is just the replacement of broth for the sauce which gives this impression.

Egg yolks are often now left on the side of the plate for the same reason. The media has told us that they are high in cholesterol and regardless of the frequency with which one might even see egg yolk in the modern Cantonese diet, it is generally left on the plate – even though the dish was chosen for the rich flavour of the egg yolk. Go figure!

In Mainland China, MSG is an expected addition to most dishes and is even served in a bowl, like sugar, to sprinkle on your food to taste. In Hong Kong, however, this is becoming less and less the norm as concern over health issues increases and many restaurants now advertise themselves as MSG-free.

Pointing

Cantonese regularly point at themselves using either the thumb or the forefinger. A different meaning is inherent depending on which digit is used. The nose is the indicator of self in Cantonese culture, not the heart as in other cultures.

Pointing at oneself with the thumb indicates pride. Yes, I did that, isn't it good! The forefinger covers the rest of the emotions, or is neutral. Yes, it's my turn, I'll take it. Yes, I did it, I'm sorry.

Just as in the West, Cantonese consider it rude to point at others with their index finger.

The little finger is used to belittle or indicate failure in others. Wriggled in the air while saying, "your English is so bad," it emphasises that an insult is intended. It should never be construed as light-hearted.

Thumbs up in Cantonese culture is indicative of excellence. The thumb is raised with the other fingers closed and the whole hand lowered to a sudden stop, rather than the Western habit of lifting the thumb, which conveys much the same meaning.

Umbrellas and walking sticks are commonly used to point at people and this should not be taken as intentionally offensive. It is merely a local habit indicating that the wielder of the weapon is trying to get a point across.

Saying sorry

A salute to the eyebrow is a gesture that means the saluter is sorry. A salute with both hands at once means you are very sorry.

You might be sorry for being late, taking up another's time unnecessarily, or anything at all. It is an admission that you were wrong and wish to make amends.

The road construction sign showing a worker in his helmet performing a double salute means, then, sorry for the inconvenience.

Pulling on both earlobes conveys a serious and heartfelt apology. The story behind this is that, as children, most Cantonese have their ears pulled by their mothers to impress upon them that they must listen and not again break the rules. The mothers might also require that the children pull their own earlobes, until they hurt, and stand against the wall as a lesson.

Step on one's toes, step on one's chest

Cantonese euphemisms for the invasion of personal space. If someone says you are stepping on his toes or chest, he is probably very upset indeed. It is unusual for Hong Kong people to make such personal comments about another's behaviour and you should take a physical step away.

If a Cantonese asks if he has stepped on your tail, he is asking if he has offended you. The expression should also be taken as apology for unwitting offence.

On the other hand, if you are asked if you mean to shave the questioner's eyebrows, he means that you are not giving him his proper and due respect. If the insult was not intended, apologise immediately.

6

OFFENSIVE QUESTIONS

How old are you?

To the Cantonese there is nothing sensitive about asking a person, male or female, young or not so young, his or her age. This is just as casual as asking about the weather but the reason behind it is quite specific. When embarking on a new relationship, Chinese like to categorise a new addition to the circle as if he or she were part of the family. The question about age, then, is to know where their duty lies: to a younger sister deserving protection, to an older brother deserving respect, etc. To Westerners, particularly women, however, the questions often give gratuitous offence.

Cantonese are starting to change in their attitudes to imparting information about their age and tend now to ask these sorts of questions in a more roundabout way: like asking what is your zodiac. As the Chinese Zodiac is made up of twelve animals, only one per year, this gives a good indication of age. Answers tend to be evasive.

After reaching about ten years of age, it is quite normal to receive the answer that this is private information and that there is no compulsion to answer the question. Cantonese accept this as an answer. If told to mind their own business, however, when asking these sorts of questions, they are generally confused and upset.

How much do you weigh?

Especially of those who are obviously fat.

In the Chinese community, this sort of query is more related to interest in the health of the person to whom the question is addressed than anything else. It is dealt with in a friendly and comparative way: "Oh, you don't look that heavy, my husband weighs the same, and he's much fatter!"

Questions of this nature are answered accurately and quite openly, it is not so much an exchange of information as mere social chatter. While a Westerner often feels that this sort of quantifiable personal information is nobody else's business and are offended by the question, Chinese are merely using the subject as a conversational tool.

Similarly, "you are looking much thinner," and "your complexion has improved since I last saw you," are not intended to be comparative with an earlier, less attractive state, but as general compliments that your life is obviously good and the benefits of it are showing.

Hello Fat Boy! *Wye! Fay Jye,* 喂! 肥仔! to a friend or stranger is not offensive to the Cantonese way of thinking. This harks back to fat being a mark of prosperity and a life of ease. The opposite of this is to call someone a dried-up monkey and that is always meant to be, and is always taken as, offensive and mean-spirited. The Cantonese is *Ma low gon,* 馬騮乾.

How much do you earn?

This is an everyday query to a Cantonese. "How much money do you have in the bank?" and "How many flats do you own?" and "How much is your rent?" and "How much does your husband/wife/daughter/son earn?" are also considered normal everyday questions in Hong Kong.

They will elicit evasive answers, often using comparatives, and (false) humility, such as "Oh, I have three flats but they are only cheap ones."

Along the grapevine of the housewives, however, numbers are exchanged in minute detail. This gossip is well intended and aimed at helping others to increase their wealth or to understand more about money.

Strangely, if a child hears his mother telling another person, even within the family, the details of his earnings he is deeply offended. He will also be offended on behalf of his brother or cousin if he hears details of that salary package or stock market coup. Most likely, this is fear of not being seen as successful or losing the comparison battle. Once this occurs the younger person may break the bounds of filial piety and forbid his or her mother from even mentioning the subject again. There is no guarantee that this will work, however!

The most popular answer to these questions is: "Not as much as you do," and this should suffice to protect anyone's sensitivities in the area.

PART III

CANTONESE SAYINGS

7

SWEARING IN CANTONESE

(see also chapter 8, forms of address)

Cantonese pay a great deal of attention to word choice. There is an underlying and pervasive effort to inject wit into daily intercourse and this spills over into swearing and other attempts to be purposefully offensive. It is a bit like cockney rhyming slang, often very indirect and based on "sounds like."

Swearing in Cantonese involves a mix of Chinese and English words used phonetically. English words which sound like Cantonese words are used to avoid direct offence – both to the speaker and the object of his vitriol. There is also a humorous intent, almost an apology for being offensive in the first place.

Hong Kong has strict censorship laws and a sub-language has grown up whereby seemingly innocuous phrases are taken to mean quite insulting things. To indicate that someone is swearing, Cantonese say that he or she is frying shrimp and dressing crab, *chow ha chark hye,* 炒蝦拆蟹.

It is not, however, light-hearted. It is meant to be taken as having been said in order to offend. Some examples of the more common usages follow.

Chee gow fa, 黐膠花, assemble plastic flowers. Harks back to the days of piecework in the early industrial era of Hong Kong. Sounds like *chee gow seen,* 黐閪線, crazy penis.

Hung ga chung, 杏加橙, apricot and orange, is taken to mean that the speaker would like to kill the entire family of the person to whom the remark is addressed.

Mo larm yuung, 冇籃用, no basket to use. Environmentalists wanted to use this phrase – it backfired because to the local ear it sounds like *mo lun yuung,* 冇𨳊用, no penis use, useless penis.

Dye ling lok, 大檸樂, large lemon coke. Sounds like *dye lun wok,* 大𨳊鑊, a big penis wok (frying pan), which means a big mess or in deep trouble.

Duung ling soy, 凍檸水, cold lemon water. Sounds like *duung lun say,* 凍𨳊死, cold to the point of death. When this drink is ordered those around may burst out laughing to cover their embarrassment at mishearing a wish for death.

Pook gye, 扑街, fall flat on the street, a total failure.

The letters PK are substituted for *pook gye,* 扑街, to soften the blow.

Nee chee PK la, 呢次PK喇, this time PK, I am in deep trouble.

Hum ga charn, 冚家剷, take a shovel to (your) entire family, I hope you all drop dead.

Ding, 頂, *ngor ding,* 我頂, fuck you, I fuck you. A direct translation is butt one's head against something. Quite polite people do not feel bad about using such language.

Ding lay gor fye, 頂你個肺, headbutt your lung (go fuck yourself). *Fye,* 肺, lung is understood to be a fusion between *fye,* 塊, a piece, and *hye,* 蟹, vagina. It would be considered just too rude to use *hye* alone. *Fye,* 肺, has become a common substitute, as the speaker does not offend himself as he is merely talking about a lung.

Deeu, 閪/屌, fuck. Used alone it means fuck you.

Deeu lay lo mo, 閪你老母, go fuck your mother. Because it is a lower-class sort of expression, the Cantonese for you is not ever said in the more refined manner of *nay,* but with the street intonation of *lay.*

Delay no more. When used as a substitute for *deeu lay lo mo,* this English phrase is taken to mean the same thing but it is considered more polite and the sensibilities of the speaker are protected.

Lay lo barn, 你老板, your boss, is a variation of *Deeu lay lo mo.*

Q is used as a substitute for swear words. *Mm Q jee,* 唔*Q*知, I don't bloody know. *Gum Q ma farn,* 咁*Q*麻煩, so damned troublesome.

Mut, 乜, what, is used as a substitute to express annoyance. *Ma farn,* 麻煩, troublesome, becomes *(jun hye) ma mut farn,* (真係)麻乜煩, (it really is) very bloody annoying.

Yeeu, 妖, demon, is used alone as a verb. It's used against others for their stupidity, not against oneself. It is taken as a sounds-like for *deeu.*

Seeu lay, 小你, little you. Used alone this gives the impression that the speaker would really like to tell you where to get off but his good manners prevent him from saying as much.

If you want to directly and personally insult someone, the personal pronoun is used.

Ngor deeu lay, 我閪你, I fuck you

Masculine

Chut, 七, seven, is used to mean the male organ but with a change of tone. It's not used alone but in combinations such as *bun chut,* 笨七, stupid penis. This is used as "bloody idiot," both as an invective against others and in a self-recriminatory manner when you feel you have done something stupid.

Lun, 閪, also the male organ. Also used as an insert in phrases so "what" becomes "what the fuck" (literally "what the penis"), *mut yair,* 乜嘢, becomes *mut lun yair,* 乜閪嘢.

Lun, 閪, can also be used as an epithet directly against the person. *Koy teeu lun yerng,* 佢條閪樣, he is a long thin penis face.

Gow, 九, nine, substitutes for *gow,* 閪, penis. It is used as an adjectival insert: *Mm jee,* 唔知, I don't know, becomes *mm gow jee,* 唔閪知, I don't *gow* know.

Ngong gow, 戇閪, feel foolish or stupid, is a rude version of the phrase, *ngong goy,* 戇居.

Feminine

Hye, 蟹, the vagina. Not used alone but with *deeu lay lo mo,* 閪
你老母, to form *deeu lay lo mo chow hye,* 閪你老母臭蟹, go fuck
your smelly cunt of a mother.

A phrase to bring it all together

*Deeu lay lo mo hum ga charn, pook lay gor chow gye, ngor do mm gow
jee lay teeu bun chut gong mut lun yair.* 閪你老母冚家剷, 扑你個臭
街, 我都唔關知你條笨七講乜闖嘢. Go fuck your mother you
motherless bastard, you total loser, I'm going to kill your whole
family, you're such a stupid dick I don't even know what you're
talking about.

8

Forms of Address

Gwye lo 鬼佬**, Gwye por** 鬼婆**, Gwye muee** 鬼妹**, Hark gwye** 黑鬼

Ghost man, ghost woman, ghost girl, and black ghost, respectively. These terms, in essence, are derogatory in nature. Whether they are intended to be derogatory depends on the tone of voice.

Some Cantonese, particularly those brought up in a less politically correct era, use the terms as a matter of course and mean no disrespect. A woman might regularly refer to her non-Chinese son-in-law, for instance, as *Gwye jye*, 鬼仔, or ghost son, and intend nothing more than description.

Gwye gwye day, 鬼鬼地, ghost ghost -ly, is an expression used to mean that the person is quite westernised or has an unChinese lack of knowledge of Chinese history and customs, etc. It is not intended to be offensive, merely commenting on a difference.

Say gwye lo, 死鬼佬

Say gwye lo, 死鬼佬, dead ghost man, is meant as an insult and is used in a third-party manner. No further action is expected, it is an expression of annoyance or disgust. If it were said face to face, the speaker is asking for trouble – it is an invitation to fight.

Westerners have found a silver lining to this ostrich-like attitude of the Cantonese to people and things they do not understand or do not like. See chapter 33 for more details.

Ga jye, 㗎仔

Ga jye, 㗎仔, ga boys, and *ga muee,* 㗎妹, ga girls, is the way Cantonese refer to people from Japan. These references are derogatory and represent the frequent use of the grammatical particle, *ka*か, when asking questions and making exclamations.

A cha, 阿差

A cha, 阿差, or *Mo lo cha,* 摩囉差, are the terms Cantonese use to refer to Indians, Pakistanis, and Nepalese. The derivation of *a cha* is from the Urdu, Hindi and Punjabi for "good" which is *"accha"*. There is some dispute whether *mo lo cha* stems from terms in Indian languages or from the Cantonese for mosque, *mo lo,* 摩囉. This in turn refers to the Islamic beliefs of so many from that part of the world. The appellations are freely accepted by the Indian community in Hong Kong when used in the third person, but are considered derogatory when used to directly address someone.

Hong Kong Chinese to Mainland Chinese, and vice versa

Cantonese often refer to their Mainland brethren as *beeu sook,* 表叔, uncle, a general term for an older male relative, *beeu jair,* 表 姐, cousin elder sister, a general term for an older female relative. This is based on the belief that Chinese are all one big happy family.

There are, however, derogatory terms in common use.

Lately, Mainlanders have come to call Hong Kong Cantonese *Gong Charn,* 港燦. The *Gong* is short for Hong Kong and the *Charn* refers to *Ah Charn,* 阿燦, an arrogant and ignorant Mainlander who was a character in a popular 1980s soap opera. The expression, then, infers that the Cantonese are arrogant, pretentious, and do not know what is happening on the Mainland which is, after all, the centre of the Universe.

Auntie, Missy

Auntie and Missy are forms of address used by Hong Kongers to address females who are not particularly well known to the speaker. Old Chinese servants in colonial households also used Missy to address the mistress of the house and her female guests.

Use of these forms of address often offends Westerners, but it is not intended to.

The choice of Auntie or Missy is based on situational factors. Auntie is respectful, recognises a generation gap, and is only used socially. The Chinese term for Aunt is *A Yee*, 阿 姨, (specifically maternal aunt). In Mainland China, *A Yee* also refers to housemaids; as use of Mandarin spreads in Hong Kong society, the term is becoming less widely used.

In Hong Kong, the transliteration into English is Auntie which is more commonly used in the middle and upper classes. The lower classes tend towards the more traditional Chinese modes of address, rather the reverse of Western customs.

Missy seems to be the preserve of sales assistants. It is a transliteration of the English "Miss." Because Chinese language does not contain a final "ess" sound, an extra syllable is added.

Missy is also commonly, and respectfully, used to address female teachers (in a similar way to *Ah Sir* for male teachers). It is always meant as a term of respect. When addressing non-Chinese, a Hong Konger often does not know whether he should attach the family or given name to any honorific. Often he cannot even tell which is the family name and which the given name, so the single word, Missy, is used as a substitute.

In Cantonese, females are addressed as *Seeu Jair*, 小姐, or *Tye Tye*, 太太, Miss or Mrs respectively. These days, women are often offended to be age bracketed, or have their marital status assumed by comparative strangers, by the use of these terms. Recently the use of *Leng Loy*, 靚女, literally beautiful girl, has sprung up to address women of any age. This neutral form of address is most commonly used by people providing services – sales assistants, hairdressers, traders, etc.

Lady

Instead of Madam. From the translation of *sook noy*, 淑女, which is the "lady" from the film title of *My Fair Lady*. It is meant as a compliment even if it sounds very odd.

Gentleman

Instead of Sir. Hong Kong Chinese call male teachers and policemen *Ah Sir*. They do not want to offer gratuitous offence, either to the person they are addressing or to any policeman or teacher who may be listening, by using an incorrect form of address. By trying to be polite, they often offend inadvertently!

Sir and Madam

Instead of Ladies and Gentlemen. Simply a difficulty of translation as in Cantonese there is only one term, *gok wye*, 各位, which is not gender-specific, means each and every one of you, and is used both in writing and in speaking.

Naming children

Chinese name their children with any one or two characters showing the expectation of the parents for the child's life, and often displaying the education standard of the parents. Better educated parents often search for an obscure word. The character may be so complex that it cannot be reproduced on normal computers.

A school teacher found a student's name on her list with a character she had never seen before. Not knowing how to pronounce it, and to avoid embarrassing herself by admitting that she couldn't read the name, she skipped it, and at the end of roll call asked, "Is there anyone I have left out?" The student raised his hand and said his name.

Mainland Chinese must now register all names using characters which can be reproduced on a normal computer keyboard. However, when a man wanted to call himself Zhao C, 趙 C, government officials refused to register the name, saying that it was not a Chinese character. In court he argued, successfully, that C is a key on a computer keyboard and so met the government requirements.

Another method is to use the given name to analyse or emphasise the family name. E.g. *Lum Joy Sarn,* 林在山, Forest is on the mountain; "Forest" is the family name and the second two characters mean "on" and "mountain" respectively, the verb is understood. *Lay Jee Huung,* 李紫紅, Plum (is) purple (and) red.

Sometimes names are a play on the sound of the characters, but not necessarily the meaning. *Gerng Chuung Ho,* 姜聰豪, means the clever and bold Mr Gerng. It sounds exactly like a delicious dish of oysters cooked with ginger and spring onions, *Gerng Chuung Ho,* 薑葱蠔.

At the other extreme, illiterate people often name their children simply with numbers, or the animals they see in their daily lives (dog, cow).

Adopted English names

When choosing a given name in English often the same rules are applied, resulting in names which sound very odd to Westerners: Gekko, Pinky, Panda, Nitrogen, Nausea, Cancer, Fanny, Dicky, Dimple, Hitler, Psychic, Hymen, Wealthee, Apple, Pear, Cream, Cookie, Pizza, Water, and Seven, for instance, are real examples of names we have come across in Hong Kong. These people are not illiterate, they know that the words are not used as names in English but are looking for something unique. If asked why they chose such names the response is generally a defensive "it's my name and you should not laugh."

Note: most names are chosen because they have two syllables and can be easily pronounced by a Cantonese speaker. Often the English names are chosen by the young person himself, although parents will choose if required by the school before the child is capable of choosing for himself. There is no thought in the Chinese community that current trends in English names need be followed.

Chinese names are not gender-specific and when it comes to choosing an English name little, if any, thought is given to the gender of the person being named. Women calling themselves Jeremy, Noel, or Toby, for instance, or men named Sue are not uncommon.

Some common derogatory forms of address in Cantonese

Fye chye, 廢柴, useless firewood, useless person.

Larn tarn, 躝癱, drag on the floor, paralysed, a useless person.

Yun ja, 人渣, human residue. Scumbag.

Jeen jing, 賤精, a cheap, mean, evil spirit, a demon.

Cheap jing, cheap 精, cheap. A very miserly person.

Say jing juung, 死淨種, die remain seed, the last person in the family. May your entire family die out with you.

Larp sarp tuung, 垃圾桶, rubbish bin, a person who eats whatever's available, especially junk food.

Lo dye charng, 籮底橙, last orange in the basket. This one is squashed or rotten, left after the better ones have been selected – it describes the bottom of the class, the loser.

Chart hye jye, 擦鞋仔, shoe shine boy, a fawner, a lickspittle.

Gum sow jee, 金手指, golden finger, to rat on your colleagues, a traitor.

Jew pung gow yow, 豬朋狗友, pig dog friends. Bad friends, unreliable.

Gun may gow, 跟尾狗, a dog follows another's tail. A follower, not a leader; a person commanding no respect.

Moon how gow, 門口狗, entrance dog, guard dog. Fierce in his own place but incapable off home base.

Fay jew, 肥豬, fat pig. Fat. Offensive. *(Fay jew jye,* 肥豬仔, fat little pig is cute, *sor jew,* 傻豬, silly pig, shows intimacy as does *chun jew,* 蠢豬, stupid pig).

Dye larn chuung, 大懶蟲, lazy worm. A lazy person.

Sook tow woo gwye, 縮頭烏龜, a tortoise with its head retracted. Sneaky, underhanded.

Lo woo lay, 老狐狸, an old fox. A cunning, experienced person.

Dye jarp hye, 大閘蟹, Shanghai crab. The live crabs are tied up with heavy string, an analogy to investors trapped in a falling stock market.

Marng tow woo ying, 盲頭烏蠅, blind fly. A person with no sense of direction, bumping into things.

Hoy luung jerk, 開籠雀, open cage bird. Keeps talking happily, like an uncaged bird, so happy it sings all day.

Woo a how, 烏鴉口, crow mouth. The allusion is to a person whose bad predictions or warnings come true, Cassandra-like. If a crow mouth person warns you to be careful of the steps, you are bound to fall down them.

Terms of address for men only

Leng jye, 靚仔, handsome man, *leng* in mid tone.

Leng jye, 嫩仔, an innocent young boy, *leng* in high tone.

Wong lo mm, 王老五, king old five, bachelor.

Jewn sek wong lo mm, 鑽石王老五, diamond king old five, rich bachelor, a good marriage prospect.

Dye jek lo, 大隻佬, *marng narm,* 猛男, muscular man, usually the bodyguard or toyboys of rich women.

Ma lut lo, 麻甩佬, someone dropping with leprosy. The meaning is archaic and no longer commonly understood. The reference now is to scruffiness.

Harm sup lo, 鹹濕佬, literally salty, wet man. A dirty old man.

Gum yew lo, 金魚佬, goldfish man, implies pederast. From a habit of promising to give children goldfish as an incentive.

Harm jew sow, 鹹豬手, salty pig hand. A man who sexually harasses women, generally those known to him.

Gow guung, 狗公, male dog. A man who sleeps around.

Gwye guung, 龜公, male tortoise. A pimp. Offensive (traditionally tortoises are good luck representing long life).

Sik long, 色狼, colour wolf. A rapist, a man. A frotteur.

Juung harng, 中坑, middle-aged man.

Lo harng, 老坑, old man.

Sew jye, 薯仔, small potato, a boring man. Sounds like *sew muck*, 薯嘜, smug, which means boring, old fashioned.

Day juung hoy, 地中海, Mediterranean Sea, descriptive of a bald head.

Gwong goon gerk, 光管腳, stripe light legs, fair, hairless legs. Derogatory, even though body hair is rare on Hong Kong Chinese men.

For women only

Leng loy, 靚女, beautiful girl, pretty woman, *leng* in mid tone.

Leng muee, 靚妹, an innocent young girl, both words in high tone.

Tye tye, 太太, *a tye*, 阿太, rich men's wives. An economically influential social class in Hong Kong. *Tye tye tewn*, 太太團, the groups in which they meet.

Yee lye, 二奶, mistress, second wife. Compared with "big" wife, *dye por*, 大婆.

Woo lay jing, 狐狸精, fox demon. A demon believed to seduce men, often used to describe mistresses.

Jew pa, 豬扒, pork chop, used to describe ugly women. (*Pa fong,* 扒房, steakhouse. Used by men or schoolboys to describe a females-only institution, school, company, etc.).

Ow woo, 丫烏, or *ow woo por,* 丫烏婆, an ugly female demon.

Fay gay cherng, 飛機場, airport (runway), a woman with a flat chest.

Mee sun, 咪神, the Breast Goddess, used shamelessly, even in newspapers and magazines, to refer to a celebrity with large breasts.

Doreen, sounds like dor leen, 墮蓮, sagging breasts.

Lo gwoo por, 老姑婆, old aunt, spinster, derogatory.

Dye seeu gwoo por, 大笑姑婆, big laugh old aunt, derogatory of a woman prone to indiscriminate laughter.

Jew la, 豬乸, female pig. A woman with many children. Offensive.

Gye jye seng, 雞仔聲, chicken voice. In singing, a soft and squeaky voice.

Ngor guung how, 鵝公喉, goose voice. A girl with an ugly, low-pitched voice.

PART IV

HONG KONG CUSTOMS

9

CHINESE NEW YEAR

This is the most important time of the year for the Chinese. Everyone stays with his or her family and a great deal of preparation and many activities are involved.

Traditions and activities
16th day of the 12th lunar month

May Nga, 尾禡. This is the final celebration of *Nga* for the year. In traditional businesses, the owner makes offerings to the Gods. A big lunch with all staff is held. For further details see chapter 16, Business Matters.

Lead-up to Chinese New Year's Eve

Barn neen for, 辦年貨, buy food, decorations, and presents for New Year visits, an outing for all the female members of the family. The most common gift is sweet snacks.

Warn sun, 還神, visit temples to pay respects and give thanks to the Gods and Goddesses from whom one sought protection at the beginning of the year. Older members of the family represent the clan.

Jeen tow fart, 剪頭髮, hair cut. Get a new look for the New Year. *Serng guung*, 雙工, double wages, hairdressers double prices in the two weeks prior to Chinese New Year.

Mye sun sarm sun hye, 買新衫新鞋, buy clothes and shoes. Shops and hair salons operate until very late on New Year's Eve. It is bargain time, with many shops (not hairdressers) offering discounts up to 50% or 60% for that new look.

23rd or 24th day of the 12th lunar month

Neen ya say jair jo, 年廿四謝灶, twenty-fourth day thank the Kitchen God. *Jo Gwun*, 灶君, God of Stove, Kitchen God, was a man who became a god after he was killed in a stove. In Heaven, he harassed the goddesses and was punished by a demotion to Kitchen God. Not much of a punishment, it suits his character because he can see women in the kitchen all day long.

Traditionally, different classes of people thank *Jo Gwun* on different days:

Goon sarm mun say darn ga ng fart fuung look, 官 三 民 四 蜑 家 五 發 瘋 六 , government officials 23rd, commoners 24th, *Darn Ga* (the Tanka tribe in Hong Kong who live on boats in Cheung Chau, Aberdeen, Sai Kung, etc.) 25th, lunatics 26th.

It sounds like a good idea to say thanks on the 26th to me, just to be on the safe side…

Two cubes of brown sugar, candies and sweet dumplings, are offered to sweeten *Jo Gwun's* tongue, so he cannot say bad things about the family when presenting his annual report on the 25th to the Emperor of the Heavenly Court. Peanuts are put out to keep his mouth busy so he has no time to gossip while at Court.

28th day of the 12th lunar month

Neen ya bart sye lart tart, 年廿八洗辣撻, twenty-eighth day wash the dirt away.

Dye so choy, 大掃除, thorough house cleaning, spring cleaning.

Decorate the house with New Year scrolls, *fye chun*, 揮春, and flowers, *neen fa*, 年花, (not white flowers, which are associated with death). Printed scrolls are sold in stationery shops and the flower market does a thriving business.

Look yow yeep chuung lerng, 碌柚葉沖涼, take a pomelo leaf bath. To bring good luck and wash away bad luck.

Some common New Year scrolls:

Guung hay fart choy, 恭喜發財, good wishes and good fortune

Fook, 福, good luck, happiness

Chut yup ping on, 出入平安, travel safely

Sun tye geen hong, 身體健康, good health

Hok yip jern bo, 學業進步, make progress in your studies

Marn see yew yee, 萬事如意, or *marn see sing yee,* 萬事勝意, everything as you would wish or better than you could imagine

Sarng yee hing luung, 生意興隆, good business

Sum serng see sing, 心想事成, may all your wishes come true

Luung ma jing sun, 龍馬精神, may you have the health and energy of dragons and horses

Fook sing go jeeu, 福星高照, may a lucky star shine on you

Bo bo go sing, 步步高陞, progress step by step

Neen neen yow yew, 年年有餘, enjoy surplus every year. This scroll may be replaced by a picture of a fish which conveys the same meaning.

Fa hoy foo gwye, 花開富貴, flower blossoming brings wealth

Jeeu choy jern bo, 招財進寶, wealth coming in

Foo gwye gut cherng, 富貴吉祥, wealth and good luck. A picture of a mandarin orange conveys the same meaning. This applies to the following two scrolls as well.

Dye gut dye lay, 大吉大利, good luck, good luck

Hoy guung dye gut, 開工大吉, start to work good luck. This particularly refers to the opening of the working year after the holiday and calls on the gods for luck in all endeavours throughout the coming year

Teen jung soy yewt yun jung sow, 天增歲月人增壽, heaven ages, people age; a wish for longevity

Chern moon keen kwun fook moon moon, 春滿乾坤福滿門, as spring is in the air may good luck come to your door

Decorations are red and gold; red, symbolic of luck, is believed to exorcise evil and gold is symbolic of wealth. Pictures of children playing, pictures of the Money God, *choy sun,* 財神, and auspicious emblems (such as fish, *yew,* 魚; bats, *fuk sew,* 福

鼠; peaches, *sow to*, 壽桃; peach blossom, *to fa*, 桃花; peony, *mow darn*, 牡丹; and an abstract design of a knot, *yew yee*, 如意), are displayed.

Fresh cut flowers and plants in bud (when the flowers bloom it symbolises the bringing in of wealth), *fa hoy foo gwye*, 花開富貴, in lucky colours of red, pink, yellow or orange fill the house. Particularly lucky plants include:

Gut, 桔 or *gut jye*, 桔仔, mandarin orange

Dye gut, 大桔, tangerine

Gum gwut, 甘橘, kumquat

Ng doy tuung tong, 五代同堂, fox face, a yellow fruit with four rounded protrusions (symbolising five generations)

To fa, 桃花, peach blossom

Soy seen fa, 水仙花, narcissus

Cherk yerk, 芍藥, dahlia (which looks like a peony)

Mow darn, 牡丹, peony, a traditional symbol of wealth

Geem larn, 劍蘭, gladiolus (not white)

Gook fa, 菊花, chrysanthemum (not white)

Larn fa, 蘭花, orchid

Ngun low, 銀柳, silvery bud, pussy willow

Many people go overseas at this time of the year, often their only chance of a long holiday. Schools and many service businesses close; offices with business related to industry are quiet as most factories shut over the long holiday.

30th day of the 12th lunar month, New Year's Eve

Neen sarm sup marn, 年三十晚, Chinese New Year's eve

Tewn neen farn, 團年飯, family reunion dinner. After a big feast and ancestor worship, visit a New Year's Eve Fair, *harng neen seeu see cherng*, 行年宵市場, more commonly known as visiting the flower market, *harng fa see*, 行花市.

The biggest New Year's Eve Fair is in Causeway Bay at Victoria Park, *Wye Yewn*, 維園. It opens four days before Chinese New Year and remains open until about 5am on first day of New Year. Half of the stalls sell flowers, the other half sell gadgets and New Year decorations. There are also a few stalls selling food and drink.

Other New Year's Eve Fairs are held in Shatin Central Park, Kowloon Park, and many public soccer grounds.

The most popular flower market on Kowloon side is *Fa Hoy*, 花墟, near Prince Edward MTR Station, this market operates throughout the year. Shops stay open 24 hours a day only over the two days immediately before New Year.

Serng tow jew herng, 上頭炷香, visit temples. The first person to perform the rites attracts particularly good luck throughout the coming year. Some people wear protective clothing, helmets and goggles, as they fight to be first and to protect themselves from the lit candles and incense held by other worshippers. Television cameras record the violence, it regularly features on the news as people fight to get their incense into the pot first.

The most popular is Wong Tai Sin Temple, *Wong Dye Seen Meeu*, 黃大仙廟. It closes during the afternoon of New Year's Eve and re-opens at 11pm, the first hour *jee see*, 子時, in Chinese timekeeping.

Soy marn sow lo, chor ng kye see, 歲晚收爐, 初五啓市, New Year's Eve turn off the stove, on the fifth day restart business. Restaurants and shops close for a few days, the owner puts a red notice on the door, telling customers when they will start business again. Generally, chain restaurants and supermarkets remain open during the holiday period. You had better book well in advance to get a seat in those restaurants which do remain open. Most business owners study the almanac *Tuung Sing*, 通勝, to choose a lucky time and day to re-open the business. Gods are worshipped and offerings laid to ask the divine powers for good luck.

New Year Activities, day by day

1st day, *Dye neen chor yut,* 大年初一

Bye neen, 拜年, praise the year; shake your fist enclosed in your other hand (it doesn't matter which hand is on the outside) as a greeting while saying something auspicious to family members and all you meet during Chinese New Year.

Auspicious sayings:

Guung hay fart choy, 恭喜發財, good wishes, good fortune, congratulations on being rich.

Sun tye geen hong, 身體健康. Good health.

Sum serng see sing, 心想事成. May all your wishes come true.

Ching chern serng jew, 青春常駐. Forever young and beautiful.

Sarng yee hing luung, 生意興隆. Good business.

Hok yip jern bo, 學業進步. Make progress in your studies.

Pye lye see, 派利是, give red packets: married couples give pairs of red packets to all children they encounter and unmarried family members. Those who are widowed or divorced, or never married, give only one red packet, as do Shanghainese and Northern Chinese.

Hoy guung lye see, 開工利是, start work red packet: Give red packets to watchman and cleaners in your building, and the waiters and waitresses in restaurants you regularly visit, as a thank you for their kindnesses throughout the year.

After a lunch at home (wet markets and many restaurants are closed), go out to pay New Year Visits, *bye neen*. Lunch is often congee, *juuk*, 粥, which sounds like *juuk*, 足, enough, satisfied, and New Year's cakes which are vegetable cakes set with agar agar or gelatine. Those restaurants that open only serve a New Year menu, have no special offers, and charge an extra 20-30% for service.

Dress in new, brightly coloured clothes, particularly red. Avoid white and grey, fashion is not important.

Cinemas remain open and gambling of any kind is good luck: *fart sun neen choy*, 發新年財. Play mahjong, *da ma jerk*, 打麻雀, play dice, *yew ha hye*, 魚蝦蟹, etc. Children are invited to gamble with the lucky red packet money.

Ho soy booi, 賀歲盃, celebrate New Year cup. An international soccer tournament is held at Hong Kong Stadium over the first few days of New Year.

Seeu pow jerng, 燒炮仗, lighting firecrackers. Firecrackers for private use are illegal in Hong Kong, but you will see them cracking away in temples and ancestral halls in villages all the same. It is a respected custom.

Fa chair chern yow, 花車巡遊, car parade, usually in Tsim Sha Tsui in the evening. Local and overseas businesses are invited by the Hong Kong Tourism Board to participate. Trucks are decorated, many hosting local or overseas dancers and acrobats, to form a colourful parade.

2nd day, *Dye neen chor yee,* 大年初二

Hoy neen, 開年, open year. Huge banquets are held at home, families pay respects to their ancestors and worship the Gods. The banquet must include vegetarian dishes, tofu coloured red, fish, chicken and roast pork. (See Auspicious Food, Chapter 23.)

Poon choy, 盆菜, basin food. Hakka-style feast food is served in a communal bowl. The dishes are layered on top of each other and each diner takes what he wants with his personal chopsticks. No serving implements are provided.

Bye sun, 拜神, praise the gods, *jok fook,* 作福, seek good luck, and *bye Tye Soy,* 拜太歲, worship the god *Tye Soy.* Visit temples to lay offerings, make wishes and ask for good luck. Every year, people of some zodiac years offend the god *Tye Soy,* 太歲. The bad luck this offence reaps is called *farn tye soy,* 犯太歲, or if the luck is seriously bad, *chuung tye soy,* 沖太歲. To avoid it, worship *Tye Soy* who is found in most temples.

Have your fortune told in a temple. (See Fortune Tellers, chapter 20.) The most popular spots are:

Sye Guung Bart Herng Chair Guung Meeu, 西貢八鄉車公廟, Che Kung Temple in Sai Kung. (Che Kung's birthday is on the 2nd day of Chinese New Year.)

Dye Wye Chair Guung Meeu, 大圍車公廟, Che Kung Temple in Tai Wai. Hong Kong Government officials attend rites at this temple to seek the fortune for the territory.

Wong Dye Seen Meeu, 黃大仙廟, Wong Tai Sin Temple in Wong Tai Sin. Especially popular as *Wong Dye Seen* grants all wishes.

Dye Bo lum chewn hoy yewn sew, 大埔林村許願樹, Wishing Tree in Lam Tsuen near Tai Po. The tree is now fenced off and boards erected upon which wishes are hung. The wishes used to be hung directly on the tree along with an orange; this, however, weighed the branches down until they were in danger of breaking.

Bo Leen Jee, 寶蓮寺, Po Lin Monastery on Lantau Island.

Marn Fut Jee, 萬佛寺, Temple of Ten Thousand Buddhas in Sha Tin.

Mo see, 舞獅, lion dances, and *mo luung*, 舞龍, dragon dances, are held throughout Hong Kong. The performers are Kung Fu school apprentices. The dances are performed on the street. The lion or dragon symbolises protection. At the beginning of the dance, the eyes are dotted and then the beast wakens and hunts for food. Speed picks up and a red packet tied to a sprig of Chinese lettuce is placed in an awkward position and it is part of the object of the dance to see how dexterously the lion is able to extract it. The pun is on the sound of *choy* (vegetables) with *choy* (wealth). The dragon need not be fed. Once he is wakened he dances playfully guided by a ball symbolising a pearl. Satisfied, the beast leaves to find entertainment elsewhere.

Yeen fa wuee yeen, 煙花匯演, fireworks, held at 8pm on Victoria Harbour. The waterfront at TST, Wan Chai and Causeway Bay is crowded. Hotels charge extra for rooms with a sea view and the Star Ferry suspends service during the performance. Boat trips can be arranged to view the fireworks from the harbour.

3rd day

Chor sarm chek how, 初三赤口, third day red mouth. Stay at home. It is said that people will quarrel when they meet.

The Hong Kong Jockey Club organises horse racing, *pow ma*, 跑馬, including a Treble, *sarm tee*, 三T. Mark Six lottery, *look hup choy*, 六合彩, is offered with an extra jackpot, *sun chern gum dor bo*, 新春金多寶, New Year snowball.

4th day

Jing yewt chor say, hoy guung dye gut, 正月初四, 開工大吉, first month fourth day, start work good luck. Most businesses re-open. The boss gives red packets (containing cash as a personal gift) to employees, *pye hoy guung lye see*, 派開工利是. This form of *lye see* is not received by civil servants as it falls outside the law.

New Year feasts are held from this day on over the first month. Among friends and relatives these are called *tewn bye*, 團拜; for companies and colleagues, *chern ming*, 春茗.

7th day

Chor chut yun yut, 初七人日, mankind's birthday. No formal celebration. According to Ancient Chinese legend, the great Goddess, *Noy Wor*, 女媧, created a different thing on each of the first ten days:

1st day chicken, 2nd dog, 3rd sheep and goat, 4th pig, 5th cow and ox, 6th horse, 7th mankind, 8th cereal grain, 9th sky, and 10th land.

15th day

Jing yewt sup ng, yewn seeu jeet, 正月十五, 元宵節, first month fifteenth day, grand evening festival. Lantern Festival, also known as Chinese Valentine's Day. In ancient China, this was the only day of the year on which females were permitted to go out in public and so the only opportunity to see females from other families (and perhaps your future wife). There is no custom of celebration amongst lovers in Hong Kong.

Huung Hum Go Sarn Do Guung Yewn Fa Dung Wooi, 紅磡高山道公園花燈會, a lantern carnival held at Ko Shan Road Park in Hung Hom. The lanterns are decorated with riddles. This had its origins in seeking a smart man to be your son-in-law.

New Year taboos, *gum gay*, 禁忌

After thorough house cleaning, bad luck is believed to be banished and good luck remains. The following activities are not advised during the first days of Chinese New Year as they could carry away the good luck:

Sweep or dust, *so day*, 掃地.

Break things, *da larn yair*, 打爛嘢.

Wash hair, *sye tow*, 洗頭. The head is the most important part of the body, these days a shower or bath may be taken but avoid wetting the head.

Use knives or scissors (for fear of injury), *yuung lay hay*, 用利器.

Use forbidden or taboo words, *gong mm gut lay gair sewt wa*, 講唔吉利嘅說話 (e.g. death, *say*, 死; illness, *beng*, 病; lose, *sew*, 輸).

Fight or argue, *da gow*, 打交; *aye gow*, 嗌交.

Buy anything associated with misfortune e.g. shoes, *hye*, 鞋 – sounds like sighing; books, *sew*, 書 – sounds like lose, *sew*, 輸, if you are carrying a book do not go near a mahjong table or you risk being chased away; clocks, *juung*, 鐘 – sounds like the end, *juung*, 終, a euphemism for death, etc.

Wear colours associated with funerals: white, black, or dark blue, or colours associated with monks and nuns: brown and grey. Colours symbolising good luck should be worn: especially red; also gold, pink, yellow, orange or purple.

New Year food

Chewn hup, 全盒, everything box. A box of mixed sweets is kept on hand for visitors, each item symbolises a New Year wish:

A pair of mandarin oranges, with leaves, for decoration, *dye gut*, 大桔 (*dye gut dye lay*, 大吉大利, good luck, huge profit);

Lots of chocolates, *jew gwoo lik*, 朱古力, and candies, *tong*, 糖, (*teem teem mut mut*, 甜甜蜜蜜, sweet and happy life);

Melon seeds, *gwa jee*, 瓜子 (*yow ngarn*, 抓銀 grab some silver/money). The grabbing refers to the action of taking up a handful of seeds which open to reveal a silvery kernel;

Crystallised lotus seeds, *tong leen jee*, 糖蓮子 (*neen sarng gwye jee*, 年生貴子, have a baby every year);

Crystallised lotus root, *tong leen ngow*, 糖蓮藕 (*gye ngow teen sing*, 佳偶天成, find a true love);

Crystallised water chestnuts, *tong ma tye*, 糖馬蹄　(*luung ma jing sun*, 龍馬精神　healthy as a dragon and horse)

Crystallised coconut, *tong yair jee*, 糖椰子　(*yair yair jee sewn*, 爺爺子孫, grandfather and grandchildren, a wish for a big family and longevity); and

Crystallised shredded coconut, *tong yair see*, 糖椰絲　(*teem see see*, 甜絲絲, sweet and happy).

Go, 糕, cakes and puddings. *Go*, cake, sounds the same as *go*, 高, tall or high, which symbolises getting ahead, promotion, growing taller, etc., (*bo bo go sing*, 步步高陞, progress step by step):

Neen go, 年糕, steamed brown sugar and rice flour cake (flavoured with coconut milk)

Lor bark go, 蘿蔔糕, steamed turnip cake (with preserved meat or mushrooms)

Woo tow go, 芋頭糕, steamed taro cake (with five spices)

Ma tye go, 馬蹄糕, steamed water chestnut cake.

Lucky New Year dumplings, deep fried snacks

Yow gok, 油角, dumpling filled with red bean paste, looks like money, gold nuggets

Gok jye, 角仔　or *choy gok*, 脆角, filled with peanuts, sesame, or sugared coconut, looks like money, gold nuggets

Jeen doy, 煎堆, looks like a full money purse (*jeen doy look look*, *gum ngun moon ook*, 煎堆碌碌，金銀滿屋, the round dumpling rolls, gold and silver fill your halls)

Seeu how jo, 笑口棗, crisp, bite-sized, doughnut with sesame coating which splits open when deep fried to look like a mouth opened wide with laughter (*seeu how serng hoy*, 笑口常開, laughing all the time)

Ja woo see, 炸芋絲, deep fried shredded taro balls. Seasonal.

FESTIVALS AND THE LUNAR YEAR

A very brief overview of the Lunar Calendar

Chinese civilisation developed using the Lunar Calendar. Many cultural activities are still held according to an almanac based on that system.

Each lunar year is composed of 12 months, except for leap year which has 13 months. Leap year occurs every four years. The leap month, set down in ancient times by the Royal Astronomer, is not the same month each leap year. One must consult the almanac to find out which month will be repeated, as any system that might have been followed in choosing the leap month has been lost. Any festivals held in leap month will be held twice during the leap year as the month is repeated.

The lunar calendar describes a cycle of 60 years, any month will only be repeated as a leap month once during this cycle.

Each lunar month is comprised of 30 days; the 15th day of the month marks the full moon.

Every 19 years, the Lunar calendar coincides with the Gregorian calendar so at age 19, 38, 57, etc., your birthday will be on the same day in both calendars.

Pay regular respects to the Gods, *Bye Sun* 拜神
1st and 15th of each lunar month

Twice each month special emphasis is placed on worship of the Gods and ancestors, both at domestic shrines and in the streets and temples. Burning incense and paper symbolic money is common, offerings of fruit, roast pork and chicken are laid in front of the shrines.

Food offered this way is left for a short time and then eaten by the family. The blessings which the ancestors and Gods bestow upon the food are thus received by the family.

Many who profess Buddhism, but are not strict vegetarians, keep these two days meat-free each month as a reminder of their faith.

> The back stairs of apartment blocks are a favoured place to burn incense, candles, and paper offerings. Back alleys and public staircases are also used to burn offerings – it is not legal but it goes on nonetheless.

Nga, 禡
2nd and 16th of each lunar month

In traditional businesses, the owners lay offerings of roast pork and chicken (*seeu yook, gye* 燒肉, 雞) to the Gods, particularly the Land God, *to day guung*, 土地公. They burn incense, and paper symbolic money. This rite is performed on the street, just in front of the shop.

The ceremony is followed by a big lunch with all the staff.

To day guung, 土地公, is the land protector, believed to guard the entrance and chase away evil spirits set on causing trouble. His birthday is on the 2nd day of the 2nd lunar month and his shrine is always at the door, just outside the shop.

The first rite in the lunar calendar is held on the 2nd day of the first month, *tow nga*, 頭禡, along with celebrations at the beginning of Chinese New Year.

The last *Nga* of the lunar calendar is held on the 16th day of the 12th lunar month, tail end *Nga*, *may nga*, 尾禡.

Gwoon Yum Hoy Foo, 觀音開庫
26th of the 1st lunar month, February

Gwoon Yum, 觀音, Bodhisattva Avalokiteśvara, is a Buddhist God imported from the Indian pantheon. On arriving in China, somehow the gender was changed and she became a Goddess worshipped particularly by women. Her areas of influence include the granting of sons, care of all people including the weak, and general wishes.

She appears in various forms, most commonly in a long white gown and veil. She may also be depicted with one thousand arms to display her power, carrying a child, or holding a vase.

Visit the Gwoon Yum Temple to perform the rite of borrowing money, *jair foo*, 借庫. Volunteers lead adherents through the ritual, a note is received detailing the amount of money that will be procured in the coming year.

At the end of the year, a thank you visit to the temple is in order. If the prediction was accurate, the amount is returned to the temple in the form of paper symbolic money which can be purchased in all neighbourhood ritual shops, *jee jart po*, 紙紮舖. When the prediction is not accurate – most of the time – a visit is still in order and the normal offerings and donations are made.

The most popular temple is in Chai Gwun Lane in Hung Hom, *huung hum chye gwoon lay gwoon yum meeu*, 紅磡差館里觀音廟. The temple is not only old by Hong Kong standards, it survived the Second World War virtually unscathed – when most of the surrounding buildings were razed in bombing raids.

The Waking of Insects, Ging Jik, 驚蟄
5th or 6th March

Also known as *jye bark foo*, 祭白虎, White Tiger Festival. The day a hungry white tiger spirit wakes from hibernation and causes trouble.

The day of the waking of insects, by spring thunder, is chosen to perform rites of vengeance, because most insects are harmful.

Rites of Vengeance

In the Guangdong area this is the best day to take revenge on your enemies, *da seeu yun*, 打小人 (hit the little man). The rite can be performed on any day of the year.

The rite consists of buying a paper effigy of the white tiger spirit and stuffing it with a piece of fat pork. The names of your enemies are then written on a special paper. Seven to eight people can be cursed at once and it works best if the birth dates are included – so that the curse will hurt your enemies more precisely.

Special ritual celebrants, or priestesses, perform this rite if you do not want, or do not know how, to do it yourself. She burns incense and offers fruit, together with the paper tiger, while chanting curses and beating the paper figures (enemies)

with your shoe. Finally, the paper is torn into small pieces and everything is burnt.

Foes are mostly workplace enemies and foolish business partners. A husband's mistresses are commonly cited as the enemies of women.

The most popular spot for these rites is under the goose neck bridge, *Ngo Geng Keeu Dye,* 鵝頸橋底, which is the local name for the area under the flyover of Canal Road in Causeway Bay. Priestesses wait in the shelter of the flyover and will quote a price for their services.

The priestess may also worship *Gwoon Yum,* 觀音, *Wong Dye Seen,* 黃大仙 and *Jye Guung,* 濟公, who are believed to be the most caring gods and goddess in Hong Kong, but the deities will not support rites which intend harm.

This rite is never carried out in a temple, only on the street and the back staircases of apartment blocks. An individual will be secretive about carrying out this rite personally against specific enemies, but not about a more general wish to curse his "enemies."

An example of a general curse follows, an individual may also compose his own curse/s with more specific details about the body part/s upon which bad luck is wished:

Da lay gor seeu yun tow, dung lay seng sye ngow ngow dow dow
打你個小人頭，等你成世牛牛逗逗
I curse your little evil head, may you be dumb your whole life

Da lay gor seeu yun how, dung lay yow jye mm sik kow
打你個小人口，等你有仔唔識溝
I curse your little evil mouth, you cannot now seduce any man

Da lay jek seeu yun sow, dung lay mo cheen jarn do sow
打你隻小人手，等你冇錢賺到手
I curse your little evil hand, you cannot now earn any money

Da lay jek seeu yun gerk, dung lay yow hye mm sik jerk
打你隻小人腳，等你有鞋唔識着
I curse your little evil feet, you cannot now wear any shoes

Ching Ming Festival, Ching Ming Jeet, 清明節
4th or 5th April

Grave sweeping, *so mo,* 掃墓: graves are tended and repaired as necessary.

It is unthinkable that a family would not perform these rites if able to do so. The importance of visits by Hong Kong families to tend ancestral graves in China is of greater significance than first meets the eye.

A paper marker at the grave testifies to the performance of these filial duties. The absence of a marker indicates either that the whole family has emigrated with no intention of return, or that it has died out. The family's land will then be resumed by the Government.

In Hong Kong, where cremation is popular and land tenure is by deed, the practice of marking graves is dying out.

Hong Kong's biggest cemetery is *Wo Hup Sek*, 和合石, in Fanling.

Flowers, roast pork, chicken, fruit and wine are offered to the spirits. Incense and candles are burnt as well as a precious basin, which contains:

Yum see jee, 陰司紙, paper symbolic money drawn on the Bank of Hell, *ming tuung ngun hong*, 冥通銀行;

Kye cheen, 稽錢, white paper slips, representative of money;

Gum ngun, 金銀, white paper, with a square of gold or silver plating, folded into nugget-like shapes; and

Yee jee, 衣紙, colourful paper rolled up to represent cloth.

Additional paper gifts which may be burnt include jewellery, cars, houses complete with servants, shirts and suits, gold watches, mobile phones, air conditioners, computers, mahjong sets, etc. Once purchased, these gifts are immediately taken to the temple and burned. It is very bad luck to take them home or keep them for later use.

Cantonese find it peculiar that tourists purchase these paper offerings to the dead as "craft" souvenirs.

Death does not terminate relationships of reciprocity among Chinese. Life after death is believed to be much the same, just conducted in an invisible dimension.

Tin Hau Festival, Teen How Darn, 天后誕
23rd of the 3rd lunar month, April/May

Teen How, 天后 is known as *Ma Zoo*, 媽祖 in Macau and Fujian.

Tin Hau, a Goddess of the Heavenly Court, is the most popular patron saint of fisherfolk. There are many legends about Tin Hau. One holds that she was a girl in poor health who often predicted danger, saving fishermen. She died young and, because of all her good deeds in life, was elevated to Goddess.

Another legend claims that in a bad storm some boatmen prayed to Tin Hau and saw her appear in the sky. The storm abated and they were saved.

In Hong Kong, thousands of boat people pay tribute to Tin Hau and there are temples dedicated to her in many places along the original coast. The MTR station called Tin Hau is named for a temple on Tin Hau Temple Road, near the station.

There is a persistent rumour that when the first Hong Kong cross-harbour tunnel was built it went straight through an area dedicated to Tin Hau. When the tunnel was completed and surveyed, it was found that the tunnel had moved to avoid running through the sacred spot.

The famous tourist market, Temple Street, is named for the Tin Hau temple on the street. The largest Tin Hau temple in Hong Kong is at *Dai Meeu Wan,* 大廟灣, Joss House Bay, in Sai Kung.

Celebrations include lion dances and parades. Boat people pray to Tin Hau for good fishing.

Tye Peng Ching Jeeu, 太平清醮, or Da Jeeu, 打醮
6th day of 4th lunar month, May

Also known as the Cheung Chau Bun Festival, it is a four-day event on Cheung Chau island. The festival placates the spirits believed to have caused storms and plagues on Cheung Chau over 200 years ago.

A huge parade is held on the second day with a lion dance, colourful flags, small orchestras, and dancers. The parade forms in front of *Buck Dye Meeu,* 北帝廟, North Emperor Temple, and winds around the island. A highlight, *peeu sek,* 飄飾, floating decoration, consists of children fantastically dressed and invisibly wired so that they seem to balance on one foot atop whirling balls, swords, or on the outstretched hand of another child.

Cantonese opera is performed opposite the temple on a specially constructed bamboo stage. The statue of the God is thus able to enjoy the opera as well as the ghosts and living beings.

The climax is the evening of the third night. After the spirits have had their feast, athletes race up the three steamed bun towers, each 50-60 feet tall, to harvest buns, *cherng bow sun,* 搶包山, grab bun mountain. Participants climb to the top to get the biggest buns, believed to be the luckiest. Buns are individually marked with a value; the competitor with the highest tally is declared the winner. A prize is offered and "copy buns" are provided to be taken home and served as offerings to ancestors and the Gods. Buns are distributed to all islanders and visitors, thus sharing the good luck and wishes for good health.

Taoist priests advise a four-day abstention from meat, and a huge banquet is prepared to share with the spirits.

The fishermen of Cheung Chau, and the Hakkas from the walled villages in the New Territories, are the oldest inhabitants of Hong Kong.

Tuen Ng Festival, Toon Ng Jeet, 端午節
5th day of 5th lunar month, June

Also known as Dragon Boat Festival, a day for family reunions. Dragon boat races are mainly held in Southern China, in areas with natural waterways.

In Hong Kong, Dragon boat races, *pa luung jow*, 扒龍舟, or *pa luung sewn*, 扒龍船 (properly called *luung jow ging dor*, 龍舟競渡) are held along the coast at Aberdeen, Stanley, Tai Po and Cheung Chau. The races function as semi-finals for the International Dragon Boat Races, held a week later.

A dragon boat is long and narrow with a dragon-shaped prow and stern. Seating between six and 20 rowers, a drummer is positioned at the front as timekeeper. If the rowers are female, the boats are built in the shape of a phoenix, *fuung teng*, 鳳艇, rather than a dragon.

Fishermen, the Fire Services Department, and many schools and companies have their own dragon boats and participate in dragon boat races on a regular basis.

Hong Kong people swim during this festival, as they believe "drinking dragon boat water" brings good luck and good health.

Mainlanders, however, avoid the water in case the ghosts of those who died in the area drag them into the underworld.

A leaf-wrapped glutinous rice dumpling, *juung*, 糉, is the signature dish of the festival. The flavour and shape of these dumplings vary regionally. In Hong Kong, it is glutinous rice blended with red beans, or glutinous rice with skinned green beans stuffed with fat pork and salty egg yolk, all wrapped in bamboo leaves in a pyramid. Sweet dumplings are made with lotus paste and served with syrup.

Dumplings with expensive fillings, abalone, wagyu beef, etc., are sent as business gifts.

The origins of the festival lie in the commemoration of Qu Yuan, a patriotic minister and great poet of the 4th century B.C. state of Chu. When he saw that his motherland had been subsumed into the state of Qin, he drowned himself in the Mi Luo River by way of protest.

Hearing news of his death, the people rowed out in small boats in an unsuccessful search for his body. They used paddles to create waves to scare away the fish, and cast sections of bamboo filled with rice into the water to feed them, so that they would not eat Qu Yuan's body.

Yu Lan Festival, Yew Larn Jeet, 盂蘭節
1st to 14th day of the 7th lunar month, August

Feast of the Hungry Ghosts: spirits of the dead are released to roam the world; the gates of hell are open during these two weeks. Cantonese are naturally very charitable and will care not only for the disadvantaged in this life but also in the next.

To appease the ghosts, who cannot feed or clothe themselves, offerings of food (tofu, bean sprouts, roast meat, fruit) are left on the street, and incense, symbolic paper money, cloth, and gold and silver nuggets are placed in a paper basin and burned. To evade strict littering laws, offerings are left in side and back streets. Foods offered are the cheaper, less desirable items; they will not be consumed later by the person offering them.

Sun guung hay, 神功戲, special Cantonese operas, are performed in open areas of villages to entertain the ghosts, the gods and the goddesses. Temporary bamboo stages and auditoria are built; the opera companies hire scaffolders to erect the structures.

Foo jeen, 付薦, a ceremony performed in monasteries, nunneries, or temples, where there is a cemetery. Prayers are said to comfort the souls of those buried there. Descendants of the deceased are informed in advance. The prayers can be expensive and are offered by professionals who must be paid for their services and have food and necessities provided during their vigil.

Boxes containing the names of the deceased, which signifies the presence of the soul in each receptacle, are the centrepiece of this rite. The boxes, which are sold by the temple, come in varying sizes and prices, the higher the price, the bigger the box and the closer it is to the action. Temporary shelving is erected to house them.

At the end of the 14-day festival, when the ghosts must return to hell before the gates close, the temple arranges for the respectful immolation of the now empty boxes.

Symbolic paper closets of clothes, money, and other gifts to improve the circumstances of the deceased are burnt.

Spectators are not welcome, the ceremonies are already overcrowded.

Since the world is full of ghosts, the whole month is cursed and no weddings should be held. People are advised not to swim in the sea, to avoid shadows in the water, and not to chase anything in the sea. It is believed that the ghosts found in water are looking for a substitute body in order to be released from hell.

Mid Autumn Festival, Juung Chow Jeet, 中秋節
15th day of 8th lunar month, September

An important day for family reunions. People finish work early to have dinner with the whole family. Married couples must either separate and go each to his own family for dinner, or, by preference, arrange that one dinner is attended at 6.00pm and the other at 8.00pm. Everyone then goes out to parks, hilltops and beaches to enjoy the full moon, *serng yewt*, 賞月. Children play with paper lanterns, *dung luung*, 燈籠, lit by candles. Traditional designs include a long colourful paper tube, star fruit, *yerng to*, 楊 桃 (the seasonal fruit), or rabbits, *yuuk to*, 玉兔. According to legend, rabbits live on the moon and make the elixir of life.

More modern lantern designs include aircraft, spaceships, tanks, animated characters, etc. For safety purposes the latest design of lanterns use plastic and are lit by battery powered light bulbs. The lanterns are tied to a bamboo stick, so they can be carried; or have wheels, so that they can be towed.

Yewt beng, 月餅, moon cake, is the signature dish of the festival. In Hong Kong, all bakeries and many Chinese restaurants produce a wide variety of moon cakes. The traditional pastry is filled with ground lotus seed paste and two salty duck egg yolks. There are varieties with none, or up to four, salty egg yolks per cake.

Shanghai moon cakes have a nut and ham filling and Chiu Chow style cakes are filled with fruit or vegetable purée, such as pineapple or taro. Ice cream makers produce moon cake ice creams, dipped in chocolate to represent the pastry. Western bakeries are more innovative, with fillings of pistachio, green tea, marzipan, wasabi, tiramisu, etc.

Pomelo, star fruit, and *ling gok*, 菱角 (a type of nut that resembles the Chinese character for eight), are the seasonal fruits to take along to the parks to enjoy while watching the full moon.

Mo for luung, 舞火龍, fire dragon dance, is performed to ward off bad luck in the Tin Hau Temple in Tai Hang, *Dye Harng Teen How Meeu,* 大坑天后廟. Thousands of sticks of burning incense are tied together in the form of a huge dragon. Twenty or more people are needed to carry this and dance on every road in the area over the evening. The dance always ends with a final performance at Victoria Park at about 9.00pm.

By contrast, in mainland China everyone stays at home; there is no celebration and no tradition of lanterns for children.

Chung Yeung Festival, Chun Yerng Jeet, 重陽節
9th day of 9th lunar month, October

Hikes are undertaken to ward off future disasters; many people take this opportunity to visit and tend graves as it is six months until grave sweeping time during the Ching Ming Festival.

According to legend, 1,900 years ago during the Han Dynasty, a Taoist apprentice, *Woon Ging*, 垣景, took his family to a high place on the advice of a sage. On returning, they found floods and sickness had destroyed everything in their village.

Chrysanthemum wine is traditional in Mainland China, kites are flown and willow branches decorate doorways; these customs are not followed in Hong Kong.

Winter Solstice, Duung Jee, 冬至
December 22, occasionally December 21

A very important family reunion day. Families celebrate with a large feast and restaurants are packed. Many offices finish work earlier, generally at 3.00pm, and overtime is avoided.

Duung dye gwor neen, 冬大過年, Winter Solstice bigger than New Year, is a Cantonese expression indicative of the importance placed on this seasonal observance. There is no celebration in Mainland China.

11

OBSERVANCE OF SPECIAL DAYS

Twenty-four seasonal lunar observances are listed in the Almanac. They are noted in local newspapers and Chinese diaries but not all are marked by particular ritual. Additionally, some Christian festivals, political milestones, Western occasions, and pagan celebrations are recognised or celebrated.

Lunar observances

Lup Chuun, 立春, beginning of Spring, near Chinese New Year, 3rd or 4th February. As Chinese New Year is a moveable feast, some years have two *Lup Chuun* (one at the start of the year and one at the end) and some years have none. Years with two *lup chuun* are lucky for births and marriages. The leap year with two *lup chuun* is the most propitious for marriage. Years with no *lup chuun* are known as *mang neen*, 盲年, blind years, and are unlucky.

Chun Fun, 春分, spring equinox.

Gook yew, 穀雨, rain for the grain, April.

Seeu sew dye sew, 小暑大暑, little heat, big heat, July.

Lup chow, 立秋, beginning of autumn, 6th or 7th August, marks cooler weather in the morning and evening.

Chow fun, 秋分, autumn equinox.

Chut jik, 七夕, Chinese Valentine's Day, 7th day, 7th lunar month. A married God and Goddess were so deeply in love that they neglected their work. The Emperor of Heaven punished them by restricting their meetings to one evening a year. The Milky Way, which in Chinese lore is composed of birds, forms a bridge for the lovers to cross for their meeting. They then return to their separate celestial positions as stars, *Ngow Long Sing*, 牛郎星, herdsman star, and *Jik Noy Sing*, 織女星, weaving girl star, for the rest of the year. Prayers and rituals are directed to the female, *Jik Noy*, for luck and good fortune in love. The rituals are waning in popularity.

Seeu sewt dye sewt, 小雪大雪, little snow, big snow, December. Snow has not been recorded in Hong Kong for over 100 years.

Valentine's Day, 14 February

Hong Kong men send flowers so their wife or girlfriend can show off to her peers. They may also give other romantic gifts – but not anonymously. The flowers are usually sent to the office and the larger the bunch and the larger the card displaying the name of the sender, the better. It is not unusual to send 999 roses, for example.

The price of flowers skyrockets, restaurants are heavily booked and hotels offer packages including accommodation and romantic extras, such as a helicopter ride over the lights of the city.

Gifts are exchanged at romantic dinners and both parties to the relationship try to find something special for their partner. Ties and wallets for men are popular as they indicate the ties of the relationship. A woman will typically put a photograph of herself in the relevant compartment in the wallet before wrapping it in pink paper.

Pink hues denote romance and either sex uses pink or violet paper.

Easter

Good Friday and Easter Monday are Government holidays. Since many offices now close on Saturday as well as Sunday, this four-day period is the longest linked holiday in the territory. Schools generally take a full week.

It is a popular time to travel as fewer unpaid leave days need to be taken.

In Hong Kong, it is a time to celebrate children. The religious aspects of the season are largely ignored.

Egg hunts are not a particular part of Hong Kong culture, but parents buy chocolate eggs, as do other family members and family friends. Schools ask parents to provide a blown egg for children to decorate.

Mother's Day, second Sunday of May

Children and husbands send flowers. Carnations are most popular. From lunchtime on, family groups treat mother to a special meal. Hotels and restaurants put up special menus.

Father's Day, third Sunday of June

Not so different from Mother's Day but less avidly celebrated. Children buy gifts for their fathers, more so than for their mothers who they would rather treat with flowers and a meal.

Establishment Day, 1 July

This day marks the handover of Hong Kong by the British to Mainland China. It is a gazetted holiday marking the end of colonial rule. It has become a day on which the public air their grievances by demonstrating.

The government also organises various activities in conjunction with the mainland Chinese government and a fireworks display is put on in Victoria Harbour.

National Day, 1 October

Not a day for demonstrations!

Government activities are organised and a fireworks display is held on Victoria Harbour.

Christmas and New Year, 25 December and 1 January

The two weeks covering Christmas and New Year is party time in Hong Kong. In Mainland China, there is a Christmas countdown on Christmas Eve but few local people know what is significant about Christmas – or even that it is a religious festival.

The end of the year is salaries tax payment time for most people in Hong Kong. Many workers receive a "13th month" salary bonus at Christmas or just before Chinese New Year.

Christmas gift giving is not a local custom and sales target personal items and clothing.

Christmas trees and decorations are put up in public places and buildings (the more vulgar the better) but decorations in the home are not *de rigueur.*

Decorations, especially along the waterfront, are put up a month before Christmas; small changes are effected after Christmas to make the decorations suitable to carry forward for New Year and Chinese New Year decorations. For example, a Santa Claus may be subtly changed to become the Money God, an angel will change into a lucky child in Chinese clothes. "Merry Christmas" will change to *"Kung Hay Fart Choy."*

Children's Christmas parties are put on by clubs, associations, schools, parents groups, restaurants, special interest groups – just about everyone jumps on this bandwagon. Gifts are provided and the parties are often quite glamorous. Many families travel out of Hong Kong once their children have been seen at these parties.

New Year's Eve countdowns are held in Lan Kwai Fong and Times Square on Hong Kong Island and along the waterfront at Tsim Sha Tsui in Kowloon. These are very popular and police security measures include blocking off roads and regulating foot traffic.

12

WEDDINGS

Couples start to plan their wedding about a year in advance. Of the many arrangements to attend to, most notable are the wedding banquet, buying or furnishing the new home, and photographs for the wedding album. One of the important initial steps is negotiation of the bride price to be paid to the bride's mother. This can be handed over at any time once it is agreed.

Negotiations take place at a meeting convened for the purpose, generally a dim sum lunch between both families. At least two, more often three, generations take part and all the expectations of the wedding are considered. The happy couple are not considered sufficiently experienced to have their opinions taken seriously, although they will be heard.

Tuung Sing, 通勝, the almanac of auspicious, or inauspicious, days for various activities (even extending to cutting one's hair!) is consulted to choose lucky dates for the various parts of the rites. Saturdays are popular for weddings and banquet halls and churches are heavily booked.

The more superstitious consult a fortune teller. The couple's birthdates are used for very complex calculations to choose the most propitious day and hour.

Approximately a month before the ceremony, the bridegroom performs the rite of *gwor mun ding*, 過文訂, exchange betrothal papers. The importance placed on this is waning, as the legal obligations of formal betrothal are defunct.

Two weeks before the wedding, the bridegroom sends gifts in the rite of *gwor dye lye*, 過大禮, passing big presents. He is attended by his brother (if he has no brother then a male relative will be asked to deputise).

Traditional gifts include:

Yair jee, 椰子, a pair of coconuts; sounds like grandfather and children, *yair jee*, 爺子. Each cleaned, empty coconut shell is painted with the double happiness character.

Bun long, 檳榔, betel (areca), the red juice is auspicious. Procurement of the betel nut used to be a hazardous undertaking which proved the love of the suitor.

Cha yeep, 茶葉, loose tea leaves, an important element. In ancient times when the bride's family accepted the offer of marriage, they said their daughter had had the tea rite: *sik jor cha lye*, 食咗茶禮.

Lye beng, 禮餅, or *ga noy beng*, 嫁女餅, cakes are distributed by the bride's family to all their own relatives, not to the groom's family. A set of traditional cakes is also bought for ancestor worship. If vouchers instead of real cakes are used, they are sent with the wedding invitation.

Other gifts are mainly expensive foodstuffs, including dried seafood, *hoy may*, 海味 e.g. fish maw, *fa gow*, 花膠, sea cucumber, *hoy sum*, 海參, shark's fin, *yew chee*, 魚翅, abalone, *bow yew*, 鮑魚, dried scallops, *yeeu chew,* 橤柱; dried mushroom, *dung gwoo*, 冬菇 , fruit, *sarng gwor*, 生果, and two bottles of wine.

Traditionally these formal edible gifts were called *sarm sung jow hye*, 三牲酒禮, three animals and wine gift, and included three live birds, a chicken, a duck and a goose. Modern people rarely carry live animals as gifts.

Kow jye hye, 舅仔鞋, shoes for the bride's brothers.

Mye gong, 米缸, a red rice container.

Jee sewn tuung, 子孫桶, a red chamber pot, because the first two words of this item signify son and grandchild.

Everything used in preparation for the wedding is arranged in pairs to symbolise togetherness.

Traditionally, the bride and bridegroom were not permitted to meet after *gwor dye hye*. Modern couples, however, complete most of the arrangements themselves and only spend the night before the wedding apart.

A week before the big day, a dinner is held to thank the bridesmaids and groomsmen. They introduce themselves and finalise their roles for the day. Contact details are exchanged and running lists given out to avoid confusion. Later the bridesmaids have a secret meeting to plot the games for the wedding – these are light-hearted teasing allowing the groom to prove his love for his bride by abasing himself.

On the eve of the wedding, the bride and bridegroom each stay at their own parent's home to perform set rites. If either is from overseas, a hotel room is rented.

Serng tow, 上頭, on the head. After showering, the bride, or bridegroom, dresses in red pyjamas, at the chosen lucky hour, *gut see*, 吉時. The designated fortunate woman, *ho meng por*, 好命婆, generally a relative, gives her blessing. This woman is a fortunate person who has had no deaths in her immediate family and is the mother of at least one son. She speaks some auspicious lines while combing the bride or bridegroom's hair with a new comb in front of a new mirror. A special hair pin, made of red string and *been park*, 扁柏, an auspicious leaf from the fire tree, is then affixed.

The usual auspicious saying while combing the hair is:

Yut sor sor do may, 一梳梳到尾, comb through the first time to wish the couple unity until the end of their lives.

Yee sor bark fart chye may, 二梳白髮齊眉, comb through second time, to wish the couple long life, until their hair and eyebrows grow white.

Sarm sor yee sewn moon day, 三梳兒孫滿地, comb through the third time to wish the couple lots of offspring to spread over the land.

The bridegroom's parents prepare the marriage bed for the couple with red sheets, pillows and quilt. Under the mattress lily bulbs, *bark hup*, 百合, lotus seeds, *leen jee*, 蓮子, and peanuts, *fa sung*, 花生, are strewn to represent a harmonious and long lasting marriage with lots of children. This food is kept for as long as possible, ideally until the birth of the first child. The family asks children to jump on the bed to bless the new couple.

In the early morning of the wedding day, the Matron of Honour, *boon nerng*, 伴娘, the bridesmaids, *jee muee*, 姊妹, and the Master of Ceremonies, *dye kum jair*, 大妗姐, who is a woman, go to the bride's house to assist her.

When the bride has finished dressing, she worships the ancestors, bows in farewell to her parents, and returns to her room, while the bridesmaids receive the bridegroom and his groomsmen.

Meantime, the best man, *boon long*, 伴郎, and the groomsmen, *dung chewn sek*, 戙穿石, or *hing dye*, 兄弟, decorate the wedding car and set out to pick up the bride.

On arrival at the door of the bride's house, the bridesmaids ask the bridegroom for a red packet, *hoy moon lye see*, 開門利是, before admitting them. Usually the amount requested is a series of the number 9, e.g. $9,999.90, because nine sounds like long lasting, a wish for the marriage in which all concur. The bridegroom must bargain and the bridesmaids must ask a very high price. The bridesmaids share the contents of the red packet.

After purchasing admission in this way, the bridesmaids play tricks on the bridegroom and his party. Various games of "torture" may include eating unpalatable food and displays of physical strength and stamina.

Often the groom is asked to make vows prepared by the bridesmaids. The most common is, "I will give all my money to my wife." In this way the bridegroom shows how much he loves the bride and promises that he will take care of her, etc. Commitment in a relationship must include financial responsibility and support of the partner's family and friends. This extends beyond household expenses, *ga yuung,* 家用, paid (generally) to the wife, even to school fees for her brothers to study abroad. This vow causes all present to nod their heads in agreement, saying, "now, that is a good husband."

Once the bridegroom passes all these tests, the bride comes out of her room to meet him. They worship the ancestors together, and, kowtowing, *jum cha,* 斟茶, offer tea to her parents, grandparents, aunts, and uncles. A special tea set in red and gold is purchased which is then taken to the groom's house, and later to the banquet, for similar ceremonies.

The Master of Ceremonies orchestrates the rites. At each stage of the ceremony the couple receives red packets, blessings, and advice, from senior members of the family. The Master of Ceremonies is given red packets at the same time. Relatives may also give gold jewellery to the bride as a personal gift.

Refreshments, particularly pairs of sweet dumplings, are served before the couple and their attendants leave for the bridegroom's house. The pair uses red bowls, chopsticks, and spoons, for good luck. These are taken with them to use through the rest of the day.

On the way to the car, the couple is sheltered under a red umbrella, upon which rice is thrown as they walk. The rice symbolises plenty.

On their return to the bridegroom's house, the couple worships the ancestors, and offers tea to his parents, grandparents, aunts, and uncles, just as they had done in the bride's house with her family. Luncheon is then taken.

In the afternoon, the couple returns to the bride's house. In ancient times, the bride returned home three days after the wedding on a formal visit to her parents, *sarm jeeu wuee moon*, 三朝回門, but now the couple returns the same day.

The bride's parents prepare a whole pig which represents the virginity of the bride and, after ancestor worship, the pig is carved and the pork distributed amongst the relatives. The head and tail of the pig should be reserved for the bride to take home. These parts represent the beginning and end, *yow tow yow may*, 有頭有尾.

In more traditional families, the bride brings home sugar cane, *jair*, 蔗, which sounds like to borrow and to lend, *jair*, 借. It represents the bridegroom's family's great wealth and signifies that the bride's family is now welcome to borrow both money and possessions.

If the civil formalities of marriage are to take place at a licensed Church or Registry Office, this is done just prior to repairing to the banquet hall. The registry offices only hold about one hundred people and attendance is on a first come first served basis, but this is not a particularly interesting part of the day for most guests. Guests should let the host know in advance whether they wish to attend the ceremony.

More and more people in Hong Kong are electing to use a Marriage Celebrant to conduct the formalities. In this case, the ceremony is conducted in the banquet hall, just before the food is served.

The Wedding Banquet

At around four to five o'clock in the afternoon, the host families arrive at the banquet location, usually a Chinese restaurant or function room in a hotel.

A reception desk is sited close to the entrance and is manned by close associates or family members of the host or hostess.

Instead of an attendance booklet, guests are asked to sign a red cloth as a keepsake for the happy couple. A *yun ching*, 人情, (see Banquets), is presented by all guests. If you are invited to a wedding but are unable to attend, you are still expected to give *yun ching*, but a lesser amount, say HK$300 instead of HK$500.

The host will stay well clear of the desk (he wouldn't want to be seen looking for gifts) but a few close friends or relations will be asked to haunt the area. From time to time they report back to the host on who has come and who has brought what. A written list is compiled of the donations and in order to do this the red packets are discreetly opened.

Relatives play mahjong as the jolly and bustling sound of the game is auspicious. A Chinese wedding must not be a quiet affair.

At about seven in the evening, the wedding cake is served and guests should have arrived by then. Similar procedures are followed as for other celebratory banquets, with some differences.

The happy couple have their photograph taken with all of the guests, individually and in small groups, for the wedding album. You might be asked to pose many times.

At eight thirty, the tables are set up and the guests are invited to sit. Seating plans are held at reception and the further you are seated from the host's table the less important you are at this occasion. The banquet generally begins at nine o'clock.

The host's table is placed near the decorations in dragon and phoenix form. Dragons now represent males and phoenixes represent females, but they used to be used only to represent the Emperor and Empress.

The couple then takes centre stage, proposing a toast and saying a few words before the serious business of eating commences.

There may be a Master of Ceremonies (a different person from she who presided over the tea ceremonies, usually selected from the bridesmaids and groomsmen) to arrange a slide show and games during the banquet. The couple plays the games on stage, and often the guests play too.

Food at the banquet is symbolic of the ideals of marriage. Roast pig, representing the virginity of the bride, should be served as the first course. Even if the couple have been living together before marriage, this custom is adhered to. It would be looked on askance if the roast pig were omitted.

When the soup is served, usually the sixth course, the host families go from table to table to propose a toast to all the guests, *ging jow*, 敬酒, offer wine.

The "brandy" with which the groom drinks the toast is usually a mixture of flat cola and tea. Some guests foist a glass of real alcohol on the groom, which good manners oblige him to accept, offering a toast of bottoms up (which again he is obliged to accept) in the mischievous hope of getting him drunk on his wedding day.

The most common dessert is red bean sweet soup (colour auspicious and symbol of love) with lotus seed (fecundity) and lily bulb (harmony), *leen jee bark hup huung dow sa*, 蓮子百合紅豆沙. A pair of sweet dumplings in sweet soup is another typical dessert.

The bride changes her outfit to show how gorgeous the wedding banquet is. Usually she wears a wedding dress and one or more evening frocks. The wedding dress may be a traditional red and gold embroidered Chinese costume, although Western-style white dresses have become more popular. The evening frocks are reddish in colour, or gold, for good luck.

At the end of the banquet, the couple and their families form a departure line to farewell the guests.

13

FUNERALS

Funerals are held at funeral parlours. Funeral parlour agents can be found in mortuaries to assist with the formalities. Ritual clothing and all supplies can be purchased from the funeral parlour which provides a price list with options for the bereaved. If the deceased or his family have no particular religious belief, the style of service is usually Buddhist or Taoist. It is not considered hypocritical to perform Taoist rites for an agnostic. The rites are dramatic and funeral parlours retain Taoist celebrants so it is also convenient.

The eve of the funeral, *sow ling*, 守靈, or *chor yair*, 坐夜, guard the soul: the body lies in state on a trolley in a glass room at the end of the funeral suite. It is shielded from view by a curtained altar in front of the glass room with curtains arranged like a diorama. A picture of the deceased is displayed on the backdrop bearing obituary comments, incense and white candles are burnt, fruit and other food (not meat) is offered to the Gods and the deceased. The funeral parlour usually arranges the offerings.

The family sits vigil all night, burning symbolic money, paper closets of clothes, and other paper gifts for the deceased to use.

The mourning dress is called *pay ma dye how*, 披麻戴孝, which demonstrates filial piety and status in the family. It is white tracksuits and white sneakers with a raw linen vest and white belt. Socks should not be worn. Mut, 襪, sock, sounds like *mut*, 密, frequent, and could be interpreted as an omen that you will attend many funerals.

Men wear a piece of black cloth on their shirt, or a black arm band, and a white headband with tails reaching the middle of the back. The widow, daughters, and daughters-in-law wear a white woven flower hair pin and a white hood of similar length to the man's headband; granddaughters of the male line wear a blue flower hair pin and granddaughters on the distaff side a green hair pin.

None of the clothing should be balanced or tailored. The tails of the belt and hood should be uneven as the desired effect is to look scruffy.

White, ecru, black, blue and green are unlucky colours, inappropriate for weddings, Chinese New Year, or any happy occasion, because they are used for mourning.

A Buddhist monk or nun, or a Taoist priest, may hold a ceremony, saying prayers to comfort the soul. The celebrants do not work alone; a Buddhist monk has a group of supporters to chant the incantations, and a Taoist priest needs a musical group to play funerary dirges. Whatever style of religious observance is followed, a Chinese funeral is never silent.

At a Taoist funeral, the priest performs *por day yook*, 破地獄, break through hell, to help the soul to reincarnate. Hell is divided into nine areas, each ruled by a king, and especially if an early death has occurred, this rite assists the soul's escape from this necessary part of the cycle.

At 7pm the room is darkened, and the priest chants rites over nine ceramic tiles representing each division of hell. The tiles are first anointed with oil which is set alight, a wooden sword is thrust into a pile of symbolic paper money, and used to break each tile, the paper falls off to add to the conflagration which, when the ninth tile is broken, indicates that the soul is released from hell.

The eldest son meantime carries a pole with a flag, cymbals are clashed, and, once the priest has performed the rites, the soul escapes into this flag. The priest then takes the flag and must run quickly around and through the broken tiles to find his way out of hell with the escaping soul. Spinning on the spot, reminiscent of the dervishes, indicates that the priest is ascending through the levels, there being no lifts in Hell.

The lights are then turned on, the priests and their assistants disrobe and sweep up the broken tiles and rubbish. The ceremonies are over.

Guests, who should dress in black, are welcome to pay their respects at any time. On entering the funeral home, visitors give cash called, *bark gum*, 帛金, silk gold, the total of which must end in one and be comprised of odd numbers, e.g. HK$101, HK$301, HK$501. The cash, rarely a cheque, is put in an envelope, *gut yee*, 吉儀, lucky ceremony, provided at the reception desk of the funeral parlour. If prepared in advance, the envelope should be white or yellow. On entering the suite, the guest gives his *bark gum* and in return receives a white envelope (*gut yee*) containing a white towel or tissue, a HK$1 coin and a sweet. Guests use the towel to wipe away their tears, eat the candy and then feel happier with their grief somewhat overcome. To avoid bad luck, the coin must be spent before returning home. A group might pool their coins to buy a Mark Six ticket.

Conversation between guests is light-hearted and not centred around the deceased. It might deal with the rites and the standard of the priests, the decorations, or the wreaths and the messages thereon.

Attendance at funerals is considered compulsory for relatives and close friends. Those unable to attend in person send wreaths with their names written clearly for all to see. A wreath might be purchased by a group of mourners. Funeral wreaths are made with chrysanthemum, white with some yellow. Chrysanthemum and similar flowers, such as daisies, are never sent as gifts.

Work colleagues, and other connections of the deceased who are not so well known to the family, might elect a representative to attend the services on their behalf. A collection is taken up to form the *bark gum*.

The family kneels on the left corner at the front of the room next to the altar.

Guests follow the instructions of the Master of Ceremonies. They are prompted to go to the centre of the room, offer three sticks of incense, bow three times to the dead in respect, and turn to bow to the family. The family then bows once in thanks, *ga sook jair lye*, 家屬謝禮, family bow thank rite, and the guests retire to the side of the room. Guests may at this stage approach the family to offer their condolences or to ask one of them to accompany him to view the body. It is polite to comment on the cosmetician's skill, the clothing on the corpse, etc. The body is generally prepared by specialists; it is most unusual for family members to be involved in the preparation.

The day of the funeral, *chut bun*, 出殯: the body is at rest in the coffin. Guests should be punctual or wait outside.

In a Taoist funeral, the eldest son (if no son then a male attendant is hired to take the role) first performs *darm farn mye soy*, 擔幡買水, carry emblem buy water, in which he walks out of the room carrying a flagpole and a ceramic bowl. Traditionally, he went to a river to fetch water. Today, the journey is to a bucket of water just outside the door.

This ceremony is another reason the Chinese are concerned to have a son to complete one's journey on earth.

Buying water is a taboo phrase. Cantonese emphasise buying a **bottle** of water to **drink**, *mye jee soy yum*, 買枝水飲, buy bottle water drink.

Towards the end, guests walk around the coffin to see the face of the departed for the last time, *jim yerng wye yuung*, 瞻仰遺容, look look remainder face.

The coffin is then covered and nailed shut. Just before this, the Master of Ceremonies reads out a list of the animals of the zodiac and the corresponding ages, e.g.: Pig 28, 40, 52. Those currently the ages mentioned should avert their gaze as seeing the coffin being covered is believed to bring them bad luck. The ages are calculated by Taoist specialists according to the time of birth of the deceased. In reality everyone turns his head against the chance that the birth time was not recorded accurately.

At the end of the ceremony, the congregation boards buses to attend the crematorium or the cemetery.

After the interment, the family and all guests repair to a restaurant for the wake, *gye wye jow*, 解穢酒, untie filthy feast. No red packet, *yun ching,* should be offered. There are seven courses to this banquet. The fare is everyday dishes, not expensive celebratory dishes.

Seven is the commonly used number for Chinese funerals.

On the seventh day after death, it is believed that souls of the dead return home for a last visit. The family prepares offerings to the ancestors, the Gods and the guards, *gwye chye*, 鬼差, ghost police, who escort souls before reincarnation. This is the last chance for a soul to review his life and the family sprinkles flour on the floor as the soul leaves footprints. The soul may return in the form of an insect; no insect should be killed in the house this day.

Every seven days after death, until the seventh repetition of seven days, that is 49 days, ceremonies known as *da jye*, 打齋, are held to purify the soul. Busy people hold ceremonies on the seventh day (first seventh, *tow chut*, 頭七), 21st day (third seventh day, *sarm chut*, 三七), and the 49th day (seventh seven, *chut chut*, 七七, or tail end seventh, *may chut*, 尾七).

14

THE AFTERLIFE

Planning for death

Older people often buy their burial plots and plan their funerals, down to the minutest detail, long before they die. The type of ceremony, whether it is to have particular religious overtones, for instance, might be specified.

Hong Kong is very short of burial plots. It may be many months before a plot becomes available if not attended to well in advance.

Traditionally, coffins were bought in advance and tended with new coats of lacquer, year after year, until needed. Coffins represented a considerable investment and the earlier they could be purchased, the better. If the family fell on hard times and had to sell the coffin, the whole family would be heartbroken.

The journey after death

When Chinese die, the guards from hell, *ngow tow ma meen*, 牛頭馬面, bull head man and horse head man, take them to be judged by the Emperor of Hell, *Yim Lo Wong*, 閻羅王.

The most desirable judgement is reincarnation as a person, less desirable is reincarnation as an animal. In Buddhist belief, 18 levels of hell exist in which the soul suffers torture ranging from a set time to eternal damnation. In Taoist belief there are nine divisions of hell in which reparation, through torture, must be made for sins committed during life.

The first step in reincarnation is to cross a bridge, *noy hor keeu*, 奈何橋, to no avail bridge. The soul then queues up to meet an old woman, *Mang Por*, 孟婆, who dispenses tea, *Mang Por cha*, 孟婆茶, Mang Por tea. Drinking the tea induces total amnesia. The soul is now ready to be reincarnated into a newborn baby.

Some Chinese stories tell of souls cheating Mang Por so they can carry memories into the next life; this is used to explain feelings of *déjà vu*.

Some stories talk of souls choosing the family into which they wish to be reincarnated. The soul may bribe the officials in hell to get into a wealthy family (the money used is that burnt at the funeral), or to be reborn as a child of your enemy and drive them crazy by behaving badly. A lover, spouse, or a child who dies young might come back in a new body.

If judged as an animal in the next life, a pig is traditionally a better choice than hardworking oxen or horses. Chinese quite casually discuss what they would like their next life to be, and what their previous life might have been. They may tease someone saying that he has died from hunger in a previous life, which is why he is so fond of eating. One may joke he will choose to become a cockroach and be killed quickly, so he has a chance to improve, whereas a tortoise may have to wait for hundreds of years.

Those condemned to hell look to the Hindu hell for an indication of their fate. Eternal hunger, being allowed only rotten and filthy foods like faeces, having one's tongue pulled (for gossiping), being deep fried, and climbing up mountains made of razor blades, all are limited periods of punishment. The lowest level is eternity in hell.

Talking about the dead

Casual chatter concerning death is a social taboo of grave proportions. Not only the words and euphemisms listed below, but any reference to death, particularly of those known personally, is frowned upon. Reference to future death generally elicits a strong and vocal reaction, "we don't like to talk about that," bringing the conversation to an abrupt halt.

A long-departed ancestor who is well known in history might be regularly invoked when introducing oneself: "I am of the 77th generation of Confucius," for instance. This is often a source of pride for the descendants, not tainted by sadness from memories of personal interaction with the deceased.

Taboo words associated with death

The word for death is *say*, 死, die. The number four, *say*, 四, sounds like *say*, to die. It is considered unlucky. To avoid talking about death, synonyms and euphemisms are used:

Mm hye do, 唔喺度, not here. If letting a caller know the family member he wants to talk to is out, Cantonese say *may farn*, 未返, not yet return, to avoid using a phrase used as a euphemism for death.

Jow jor, 走咗, has left, gone. Don't use this phrase to refer to a middle aged or elderly friend who has migrated!

Farn herng ha, 返鄉下, return to one's homeland. Again, if talking to the elderly about a trip to his homeland, use the actual name of the homeland to avoid unintentional offence.

Herng jor, 香咗, incense burnt, refers to the practice of burning incense at a shrine to commemorate the deceased.

Harm yew, 鹹魚, salty fish, Cantonese slang for corpse.

Mye harm ngarp darn, 賣鹹鴨蛋, selling salty eggs. This harks back to Taoist funeral rites of painting a salty egg with the face of each of the nine kings of hell in the *por dye yuk* ceremony. This detail of the rites is dying out but the linguistic proscription remains.

Hem jor, 鹹咗, dialectic (Hakka) rendering of *harm*, salty.

Gwa jor, 瓜咗, decomposed.

Gwa lo chun, 瓜老襯, decomposed in-laws, a colloquial variation of *gwa jor*.

15

CHINESE BANQUETS

Formal banquets are hosted by Hong Kong Chinese to mark certain family events, notably weddings, births, and birthdays.

Hoy yum, 去飲, go to drink, means go to a banquet. This saying persists even though very few Hong Kong Chinese drink alcohol as many suffer from an allergy to it. A lack of the enzyme needed to digest the alcohol results in a bright red face, nausea and dizziness.

Bye jou, 擺酒, lay out alcohol, is an invitation to a banquet. You should arrive at least an hour before the banquet starts (generally 8.30–9.00pm). In Hong Kong, banquets are held only in the evening but in Mainland China banquets may be held at lunch or early evening, that is at 6.00–7.00pm.

Guests are seated at round tables of twelve.

Red packets

Yun ching, 人情, people sentiment, red packets. On arrival, guests find the host and present a red packet containing cash or a decorative bank cash cheque.

The going rate is HK$500 (US$65) per person. The immediate family of the host does not give *yun ching* but close family members, uncles, aunts, adult children, generally give more. The overriding thought behind the gift is to pay for your own meal, and the amount has remained the same for many years.

A gift is not expected on top of the red packet, but it is not wrong to give one. (See chapter 17, Gift Etiquette).

People may be financially embarrassed and unable to settle the restaurant's account at the end of the function without these red packets.

Lye See, 利是, the host prepares envelopes of cash for each guest. The *lye see* is presented personally by the host; the sum need not be large, it is a gift of luck. The host may need to check whether the guest has already been given an envelope and the question is asked and answered without a hint of discomfiture. Sometimes this red packet is sent with the invitation card.

Food at the banquet

There are generally eight or nine courses. Only at funerals are seven dishes offered. If you are vegetarian, you should inform the host who will make special arrangements – no strictly vegetarian food will otherwise be served.

Formal dishes for entertaining and banquets are never vegetarian. There is always some seafood, meat, or fowl, product included in the preparation. Lard is often used for cooking although this trend is weakening in Hong Kong's social climate of strengthening health consciousness. Chinese vegetarians include garlic and spring onion on their taboo list. It is a nightmare for the chef who has no way of knowing what might be considered vegetarian by any particular diner.

The first course is a platter of barbecue meats with jellyfish; at banquets that are more expensive, you might start with a whole

suckling pig. The eyes will be represented by cherries or battery operated red light bulbs for effect in the "parade of dishes." The waiters form a line and walk around the banquet hall, displaying the food they are about to serve.

The second to fifth courses are cooked dishes of various vegetables and seafood, abalone with lettuce, prawns and cashew nuts, melon rings with dried scallops, etc. Most dishes are chosen because they carry auspicious meanings. (See chapter 22, Auspicious Foods).

The sixth course is soup, most commonly shark's fin. Fin in Chinese is the same word as wings and the appeal of this is the thought that the host will take off to success – like an eagle spreading its wings in flight.

Ging jow, 敬酒, respectful alcohol, a toast to the guests. When the soup is served, the host goes from table to table proposing toasts to the guests.

The toast is supposed to be offered in alcohol but as so many Chinese are allergic, the restaurant, if asked, will prepare a mixture of Coca Cola and tea and leave it to go flat until it looks like brandy. Guests return the toast in their tipple of choice – table wine, tea, water, soft drink, etc.

Yum booi, 飲杯, drink the glass, is the toast offered. In the old days, the form was to hold the glass with both hands, lift it in offering, and drink the contents in their entirety. The more modern practice still requires two hands as a formal gesture but you are not expected to finish the glass for each toast.

The host may offer more than one toast to the table. The first toast will be offered to all of the guests at the table and if any guests are especially enthusiastic towards the host, he may offer personal toasts to them or to small groups at the table. The guests may also propose individual or group toasts to the host and his party.

The seventh and eighth courses are deep fried chicken followed by steamed fish. The chicken and fish must be whole, complete with head and tail, emphasizing completeness. Chicken represents the phoenix, a legendary bird that means the host will take off to success. The fish represents surplus.

Dong huung ja jee gye, 當鴻炸子雞, now good luck deep fry young chicken, whole fried chicken: *huung,* 鴻, good luck, sounds like *huung,* 紅, red; it is a play on words between "red dish" and "good luck dish", giving Cantonese speakers the pleasure of two, or even three, word plays for the price of one of the same kind.

The second to last course is staples, such as fried rice, noodles or dumplings.

The final course is dessert and fruit. Two types of dessert are always served: a sweet soup and a plate of petit fours. The fruit is often oranges, served whole because they look like balls of gold.

Behaviour at the banquet

Hay fye, 起筷, lift the chopsticks, is said before starting to eat.

Yum booi, 飲杯, drink the glass, is said before each dish.

Guests feel free to comment on the food and compare it with other banquets they have attended. It is not rude to say the food is no good; Chinese think they have paid for their own meal by presenting a red packet.

Most restaurants have the waiter serve onto individual plates. When this is not the case, the guests serve each other. Do not serve yourself first, as that is considered very rude.

Lazy Susans: a revolving stand in the middle of the table on which the waiter puts the dishes. If he serves, he will stand at his station (at which serving tools have been laid) and either hand out the plates to individuals, or put them on the perimeter of the Lazy Susan.

If the waiter leaves the dishes on the Lazy Susan, the guests decide amongst themselves who is to start first and this may change from course to course. For instance: young people first, ladies first, you're the closest, etc. Remember to always serve a plate to someone else before taking your own.

Serng choy wye, 上菜位, up food place; or *chut choy wye,* 出菜位, out food place, is the waiter's service station.

There is a legend behind a persistent joke which plays on the words of the serving station. Historically, one of the four beauties of Chinese history was sent outside China in marriage. Her story is known as *cheeu gwun chut choy*, 昭君出塞, and, instead of saying *chut choy wye*, 出菜位, to describe the waiter's station, people get a kick out of saying *cheeu gwun wye*, 昭君位 (beauty station), instead.

The depth of this joke is very typically Cantonese. Note that the two words of the title which sound like the two words that describe the station are not pronounced; the other half of the title is used and the word for station, *wye*, is added at the end.

Before the waiter takes away each dish, he serves any remaining food, asking which guests want extra.

Surplus food is taken home. Particularly, the oranges served at the end of the banquet. Often plastic bags are provided for this purpose on the table at the same time that the dessert course is served. By then most of the guests are sated and would rather take them home than deal with the often messy task of peeling an orange with a restaurant knife.

The host will be informed by the kitchen of the amount of leftover food which is packed up to take away. It is packed according to type so all the chicken is in one set of boxes, all the pork in another, etc. Any remaining oranges will just be heaped in plastic bags. The host will then order the distribution of the food, generally among his close relatives.

Leaving the banquet

The host and his party line up to farewell the guests at the exit. They make their way to the entrance just as the dessert is brought out. The moment oranges are served is the signal for guests to take their leave.

Wedding banquets

See chapter 13, Weddings.

Birthday banquets

Bye dye sow, 擺大壽

Men celebrate their birthday with a banquet at the ages of 60, 70, 80, 90, etc. For women, it is 61, 71, 81, etc.

Food is ordered according to the host's tastes with one exception: dessert is always a steamed bun shaped like a peach. (See chapter 22, Auspicious Foods).

Gifts: you are not expected to buy a gift on top of paying for your meal at the banquet in the form of a red packet. (See chapter 17, Gift Etiquette, Birthdays).

Newborn baby banquets

Bye moon yewt jow, 擺滿月酒

Held when the child reaches one month old, to present him or her to family and friends. No special foods are served at the banquet although there may be traditions within families which dictate certain dishes.

Leaving school banquets

Jair see yin, 謝師宴

Students in the last year of school arrange a banquet to thank their teachers. All the students invite all the teachers. The banquets are famous for the economical choices made on the menu. Hotels and restaurants tend to be generous, offering a low priced but plentiful menu, and students try to find as smart a place as they can afford. No doubt, it is all good marketing!

16

BUSINESS MATTERS

Grand Openings

An auspicious time is chosen for the grand opening of a business. This need not be the day the business actually opens, it may be earlier or later. Almanacs and fortune tellers are consulted to select the right moment, taking into account the personal particulars of the owner.

Rituals on opening include the burning of incense and the consumption of Roast Suckling Pig as an offering to the gods. If you are vegetarian or have religious food prohibitions, stay away! A refusal to eat this lucky dish may offend.

No matter what type of business is being opened, a ribbon-cutting ceremony will be performed. The greater the celebrity of the scissor wielder, the more attention that can be attracted, the better. A dragon or lion dance is often performed to attract good luck and frighten away evil spirits. Firecrackers are also let off, with (or without) Government permission.

An open house follows. This lasts all afternoon and refreshments are offered. The first customer follows closely on the heels of the open house, generally organised by the new business owner. *Fart See*, 發市, prosperous market, is the name given to the process of serving the first customer.

Well-wishers send floral arrangements, usually presented on a stand at eye level. Either an oversized gift card or a broad ribbon, stating the names of the givers in large print, is attached so that passers-by can immediately see who in the industry supports the new venture.

An array of gifts might be given by those close to the new business owner, particularly for new shops. After lucky cats, toons (statuettes of animated characters, usually carrying boxes of gold to attract more money) are the most popular.

Lucky statues and altars

Jeeu choy mow, 招財貓, lucky cat – with a paw in the air. The left paw in the air signifies bringing in customers, the right paw brings in money.

Altars: may be to *Gwarn Guung* 關公, *Gwoon Yum* 觀音, Bodhisattva Avalokiteśvara, *Fut* 佛, Buddha, or a host of other deities. *Gwarn Guung,* based on an historical character, is the God of War. Always facing the entrance, he wards off demons and evil spirits and is the protecting deity of restaurateurs and money-changers, among other trades. *Gwarn Guung* is also patron of the military, the Hong Kong Police (especially the Criminal Investigation Department) and is guardian spirit of all brotherhoods.

To Day Guung, 土地公, the Land God: in front of retail outlets and restaurants, a small, altar-like, permanent arrangement is located for laying offerings. It is always to the side of the front door, often at an angle facing the door opening when placed outside. If inside, it is directly inside the door, off to one side at the closest convenient juncture of the floor and wall. *To Day Guung* wards off evil spirits.

In front of the shrines, incense is burnt and fruit laid. On altars, a pair of red candles are these days replaced with flame-shaped light bulbs. These should not be turned off and are called *Cherng Ming Duung,* 長明燈, long bright light.

Ngar, 禡
2nd and 16th of each lunar month

Traditional ceremonial offerings include the burning of symbolic paper money. (See chapter 10, Festivals and the Lunar Year).

General business gifts

See the following chapter 17, Gift Etiquette.

17

Gift Etiquette

General gifts

Lye see, 利是, meaning 'is of benefit', describes a red packet which is suitable for any occasion to wish good luck. A red packet is a special envelope, *lye see fuung,* 利是封, benefit envelope, into which banknotes are put. The envelopes are readily available at stationers and at the counter of most Chinese restaurants. The newer the banknote the better, the amount is up to you. There is no shame attached to putting a small-denomination note in the packet for good luck, it depends on the occasion, the relationship, and, to a lesser extent, the financial status of the giver.

In place of a birthday gift, the amount would be what the giver is prepared to spend on a present. If to wish good luck with exams, for instance, the luck is conveyed by the packet, not the value of the note inside; common practice dictates a nominal HK$20.

Wallets and bags are good choices as lucky gifts. The Chinese saying, *doy doy ping on,* 袋袋平安, may the wallet be stuffed with money and may you be safe and secure, will automatically be associated with the gift.

Other good general gifts include gadgets, accessories, jewellery, toys, etc., much the same as Western gifts. Watches, necklaces, bracelets, rings, ties, belts, etc., in fact anything which is fastened around the body, are gifts indicating a close relationship and should not be chosen for a casual acquaintance or work colleague.

Colours: pink, red, yellow, orange, and purple are considered happy colours. They are much preferred to white, black, grey, blue, green, or brown which can be associated with funerals and poverty. Blues and greens are acceptable in bright and light tones.

Amongst the Chinese, it is peculiar to Hong Kong that animated characters are considered cute, and suitable as gifts for people of all ages. A middle aged woman will carry a Hello Kitty wallet or wear a Winnie the Pooh T-shirt without embarrassment. Hello Kitty on a lucky pink or red background and the fat cuddliness of Pooh are particularly appealing. Men tend towards animated action characters like Spiderman, Keroro, Ultraman, etc.

Statuettes of animals, mythical or otherwise, are tricky. Great care needs to be exercised, as some are considered proper only for tomb adornment, and others are endowed with mythical powers too strong for domestic purposes. Careless display of such power can lead to householders feeling uncomfortable as they are seen to be attempting to harness a power more properly in the realm of the Emperors or the Immortals.

Statues of Buddha, the Immortals, Gods and Goddesses, etc., should be avoided.

Gift taboos

Clocks, books, and shoes are associated with misfortune and should not be given as gifts.

Juung, 鐘, clocks, sounds like *juung*, 終, the end. The act of presenting a clock as a gift, *suung juung,* 送鐘, sounds like *suung juung*, 送終, see one's father die.

Specifically taboo for Cantonese speakers:

Sew, 書, books, sounds like *sew*, 輸, to lose. Not a good choice for a family that likes to gamble or to win. Some families go so far as to refer to books as *yeng*, 贏, win, to avoid using a bad luck term.

Hye, 鞋, footwear, shoes, slippers, sandals, sneakers, etc., sounds like *hye* (no character), sighing in Cantonese. It is also considered strange to send a gift to be trodden on.

House gifts, hostess gifts

Normally food, especially fruit or sweet things, is acceptable, or, if you know your host drinks alcohol, a bottle of wine. Expect a red packet in return. This can be handed to the guest at any time before he or she leaves. All householders keep a supply of the special envelopes on hand and the value enclosed will depend on the value of the gift.

In Chinese society, the circumstances of the recipient are the driving factor in the choice of gift. What will he use? What does he need? It is considered thoughtless to give a poor man a bottle of expensive cognac. Not only is it seen as showing off your greater wealth, he also loses face as he must either make serious sacrifices to give a sufficiently large red packet in return, or give a red packet which is insufficient.

The gift is presented in the wrapping from the shop. This gives an indication to the canny hostess of the value of the gift, enabling her to prepare a suitable red packet in return.

Younger Chinese open the gift in front of the giver, but people who are more traditional never do. They thank the giver politely and put the wrapped gift to one side to deal with later. It is considered rude to open the gift in front of the giver as your face may show an emotional reaction which could give offence. No card is attached to the gift.

As a dinner guest, if you have specific dietary requirements or are vegetarian, it is acceptable to take your own food. Very few Chinese are strict vegetarians and are often confused by its various forms. For this reason, Chinese hosts are relieved to have the decisions taken from them; they are not offended in any way if the guest brings his own food. The host should, of course, be informed that he need not cater for you. It might be a good idea to take a little extra. Chinese are naturally curious about food and are willing to try new tastes and preparation methods with little encouragement.

When entertaining children, do not be surprised if their parents provide food, especially snacks. It is considered "sharing" and is not meant to be offensive in any way, nor to suggest that the child would otherwise go hungry in your house.

Banquet gifts

A red packet or gift cheque (purchased from a bank) is presented on arrival. This only applies to personal invitations, not business banquets.

The going rate is HK$500 per person but guests with a closer relationship (uncles, aunts) give more money. The thought behind the gift is to pay for your own meal; it has remained at the same level for many years. If the banquet is held at a five-star hotel or other expensive restaurant, the amount paid should be increased accordingly.

At banquets for weddings, birthdays, births, etc., it is quite acceptable for a number of guests to purchase an expensive gift jointly. A gift is not compulsory, you are already paying for your place at the banquet.

Wedding gifts

The same rules of choice apply as to Western customs. The gifts should be delivered before the wedding banquet, to the bride's parents' house or at her directions.

Choosing the gift: household appliances or jewellery are very popular. It is quite proper to ask the couple directly what they want. Normally, Chinese do not issue a list. They see this practice as asking for a gift and would be embarrassed to do so.

Traditional gifts: gold bracelet or necklace with patterns of phoenix and dragon (harmony) or pig with piglets (fecundity). Sent by older generations of the bride's family, the gift is to the bride and becomes her personal property, not the property of the marriage.

Personal gifts to the groom are not common.

Taboo gifts: any image of butterflies. Butterfly images are considered unlucky because of their association with the great tragedy, *Lerng Sarn Bark Yew Jook Ying Toy*, 梁山伯與祝英台, the Butterfly Lovers. The story has an unhappy ending with the girl, *Jook Ying Toy*, 祝英台, committing suicide by jumping into the grave of her lover, *Lerng Sarn Bark*, 梁山伯. The tomb then explodes, the lovers being turned into butterflies.

Birthday gifts

Same as Western customs, anything that suits the interests of the recipient.

Within the family, a hard boiled egg, dyed red, represents a wish that the recipient have a lucky life. Eggs represent life and eating the red egg signifies that you accept the good wishes of your family.

Traditional gifts: gold peach-shaped ornaments, not jewellery, for significant birthdays, 60, 80, etc. Chinese jewellery shops stock a wide range.

Newborn gifts

Same as Western customs: clothes, toys, etc. Deliver them to the mother or the house at the first visit after the birth.

Traditional gifts: bracelets for wrist or ankle in gold, silver, or jade. Jade is believed to offer protection from demons and to confer peace on the baby. When the baby grows, jade bracelets have to be broken to be removed. Jade pendants are a less common gift for newborns.

Thanks for the gift: the new mother or her family prepares *gerng cho*, 薑醋, a dish made from sweet dark vinegar, ginger, pork knuckle, and egg. This is offered to first-time guests. It is also taken out into the community by the new mother and mother-in-law to spread the good news and share the joy.

Originally, *gerng cho* was made for the new mother as a nutritious supplement but it has become so popular that it is offered on the menu in some dim sum restaurants.

Business gifts, to or from a business

General business gifts: food – the more elaborately packaged and the more expensive the better. Avoid any food which is fragile, such as custard tarts; perishable, such as roast goose; or smelly, such as cured ham. These gifts are not completely taboo, they are eminently suitable for relatives or close friends, just not for business.

At Chinese festivals: food is the expected offering. The more expensive the filling in the various food items, the better.

Packaging is included in calculating the importance of the gift and can be very elaborate indeed.

Chinese New Year: bakeries and Chinese restaurants produce New Year's cakes, often in the shape of carp, *gum lay*, 錦鯉. Edible gold leaf and red dates are popular decorations.

Dragon Boat Festival: rice dumplings with expensive fillings of abalone, foie gras, etc. Red bean or pork fillings are also made for personal consumption or gifts to relatives, not for business purposes.

Mid-Autumn Festival: Moon Cakes in decorative boxes. The more egg yolks in the filling the more desirable (and the more expensive).

Christmas: gift baskets in the Western style, often including wine, chocolates, and tinned gourmet products.

Grand Opening gifts: See chapter 16, Business Matters.

Visiting the sick

When visiting the sick, either in hospital or at home, gifts like nourishing foods are expected.

At the top of the list is home-made soup. Power drinks, bottled ready-to-eat bird's nest and chicken essence follow closely behind.

Magazines are a thoughtful gift showing that you understand the need to keep up with the gossip and that heavier reading may not be possible.

The Western habit of a bunch of grapes or flowers is also welcome, but if the friendship is a close one, it might be considered a little insensitive. Many Chinese avoid giving flowers in this situation as the pollen may cause allergies and the scent in an enclosed space can be annoying.

PART V

RELIGIOUS PRACTICE

18

RELIGION – CANTONESE STYLE

Most Hong Kong Chinese honour their ancestors in some way. This is not considered religion but is seen as further contact with deceased family members. There is a common belief in an afterlife in which the deceased remain influential in everyday matters and exist on earth in an overlapping dimension.

Even though all the hallmarks of religion are present: prayer, pilgrimage, propitiation, appeasement, ritual, offerings, and a belief in the immortality of all who have gone before, Hong Kong Chinese fiercely deny that it amounts to religion. It is described as "paying respects." In this book, we use the term "worship" for want of a more convenient term.

Whether ancestor worship is in addition to other forms of worship, or is just empty observance so as not to offend living members of the family, is a matter for the individual.

Few Cantonese actually profess to "belong" to any religion; they engage in acts of ancestor worship as family cultural activities.

Bye jo seen, 拜祖先, ancestor worship

Each household sets up a shrine to the ancestors. This is usually set up serially with a shrine or shrines to the Gods (which take precedence) and lesser shrines to individual ancestors, generally the more recently departed. Female ancestors are not named in full, just as an adjunct to her husband with her maiden name shown but not her given names.

The ancestors' shrines command the same respect as those of the Gods and are placed in the living room at eye level. An incense container is placed at the front of the shrine along with a plate of fresh fruit and often a vase of flowers. A picture of the deceased or a tablet with Chinese characters describing the family and its ancestors forms a backdrop.

Daily: pay respects morning and evening to the Gods as well as to ancestors.

First and 15th of each lunar month and festival days: special emphasis is placed on paying respects to the Gods at domestic shrines. Burn incense and symbolic paper money, lay offerings of fruit, roast pork and chicken in front of the shrines. The offerings are intended to be shared by the ancestors and Gods.

Food offered this way is left for a short time and then eaten by the family. The blessings bestowed upon the offerings by the ancestors and Gods are then received by the diners.

Vegetarianism, *sik jye*, 食齋, is practised by some people on these two days. It is a good idea to book in advance if you want to be assured of a seat in a vegetarian restaurant.

Ancestral Halls

Each village has an Ancestral Hall for ancestor worship. They were originally built under strict guidelines. The sponsor had to be a man of or above a certain rank, and the rank dictated the size and style of the hall. Upkeep is funded by the community.

The hall is sacred and contains a wall of wooden placards in memory of the departed. Offerings are laid and ceremonial rites are carried out regularly. When important matters concerning village life need to be discussed, the discussions take place in the hall.

Only men may enter an Ancestral Hall – even today. The parish records are kept in the hall, for men only. Women are not seen as having personal identities; in records they exist as wives. Unmarried daughters traditionally brought shame onto their fathers.

Visitors are not welcome.

Temples

Most people visit temples at the beginning of Chinese New Year as a family outing. The first two or three days are best and questions cover general conditions of the year to come as well as general concerns about *jee sun*, 自身, oneself, *ga jark*, 家宅, family, *see yeep*, 事業, career, or *yun yewn*, 姻緣, love and marriage.

Meeu Yew Wye Yewn Wooi, 廟宇委員會, the Chinese Temples Committee, governs all matters pertaining to temples. The organisation is funded by public donation. There are collection boxes in each temple and worshippers make a donation as a matter of course whenever they visit the temple.

Temple visits are undertaken at any time of any day. The purpose is to lay offerings, express wishes, ask for good luck, and seek divine intervention with personal problems.

Many temples have resident fortune tellers who occupy an official desk in the environs.

Pantheism

There is a huge number of Gods in China. They each have their divine duties and may be historical figures deified or figures from literature and myth.

Most temples house many gods, sometimes from different religions. Wong Tai Sin Temple, for instance, has a Buddhist shrine, a Taoist shrine, and a Confucian shrine within the environs. Cantonese tend to worship all of the deities when they visit the temple.

The Gods can be invited to visit another temple or even to come home with you to your domestic shrine. Certain rites must be performed and once the God arrives at the new destination, he splits his personality (but not his power) and then resides at both places. Che Kung Temple, *Chair Guung Meeu,* 車公廟, originally in Sai Kung, now also resides in Tai Wai by invitation.

Some temples or shrines are famous for a particular purpose. Man Mo Temple on Hollywood Road is prayed to for passing examinations; Lover's Rock, *Yun Yewn Sek*, 姻緣石, on Bowen Road is appealed to for true love.

The Gods are in addition to conventional world religions which abound in Hong Kong. Churches, temples, mosques, and synagogues are all present, running the gamut of religious disciplines from Abrahamic to Zoroastrian.

19

FORTUNE TELLERS

Fortune tellers in Hong Kong work out of established offices and there is a mall of fortune tellers at Wong Tai Sin Temple. Some fortune tellers use one method to predict or advise, some use another, or a combination of methods. The main areas and means of prediction follow.

Predicting the future

Sewn meng, 算命, life calculation. Study of the exact time of birth.

Tye serng, 睇相, read the face. Interpretation of the juxtaposition of facial features.

Tye jerng, 睇掌, palm reading. Interpret life through study of the lines of the hand.

Sewn Meng practitioners mainly use three methods: *Teet Barn Sun So*, 鐵板神數, calculating on the abacus, *Jee May Dow So*, 紫微斗數, calculating the stars, and *sarm sye sew*, 三世書, three lives book.

Teet Barn Sun So refers to the exact second of birth. Minute calculations foretell the events in each year of life. At present, there is only one master of the discipline but he does have disciples and people come from the far corners of the earth to consult them.

The readings are indefinite and are based on a word or phrase which must be kept in mind so that if it is a bad omen steps can be taken to lessen the impact of, or even avoid, the disaster. When the years are without event, this indicates the end of life.

A typical warning might be *yut jee gay jee yerk teen, ga but duck*, 一字記之曰田, 嫁不得, one word written down as *teen*, 田, should not marry. A prediction that marriage with anyone named *Teen* will not be harmonious.

Jee May Dow So refers to the arrangement of the stars at the exact moment of birth and the effect that this will have on the rest of life.

Sarm sye sew is a reading of deeds in the previous life which affects not only this life but also the next.

Tye Serng, 睇相, face reading. Most Chinese have some concept of face reading. The forehead and ears tell about childhood, the area around the eyes and nose refer to middle life, the mouth and chin the later years.

If a child has a protruding forehead and long or well-shaped ears, he is assured of a happy childhood and this in turn brings good luck to his parents.

Watery (sparkling) eyes are said to attract the opposite sex and laugh lines, particularly in men, indicate promiscuity. A superabundance of white of eye indicates sex mania and small eyes indicate hardworking character traits.

The size of the nose is said to be relative to the size of the penis.

In women, a fleshy nose combined with high cheekbones means she will bring wealth and good luck to her husband.

A lantern jaw is indicative of retention of wealth into later life and a downturned mouth combined with a receding chin predicts an unhappy or uncomfortable old age.

A square face indicates a traitor and this person is not to be trusted. Slender-shouldered people cannot be trusted with responsibility and low-waisted people are lazy.

Thick palms indicate a good life and, if a gap shows between the fingers when they are pressed together, money will flow out through the gaps.

> Parents are quick to point out any character flaws based on this method when they first meet their children's boyfriends and girlfriends.

Jark yut, jark see sun, 擇日, 擇時辰, auspicious timing

Various areas such as grand openings of shops or new businesses, moving house, thorough house cleaning (particularly before Chinese New Year), haircuts, travel, surgery, etc., are all areas in which advice might be sought as to timing. The *tuung sing* 通勝 almanac (better known as *tong shu*, 通書, which is its Mandarin name) is consulted to select an auspicious day or hour. Some people read the almanac for themselves, others consult a fortune teller. Daily newspapers and some Chinese websites give details of the events that would be auspicious on that day, though this does not help with advance planning.

Weddings: particularly when there is some question of the suitability of the pairing, a propitious time is sought to counter negativity. Both the date of forthcoming nuptials, and sometimes choice of partner, is sought. Fortune tellers study the times of birth of the couple which also indicate whether the marriage will be a happy one: *garp see sun bart jee*, 夾時辰八字, match hour match elements. A bad prediction might be countered by following certain advice.

Births: advice is sought on the exact time of birth. Caesarean section is more and more popular to comply with the detailed time requirement so that the child might have the best possible future.

Fuung Soy, 風水, wind and water, Feng Shui

Advice on rent or purchase of an office or residence might be detailed down to the arrangement of furniture, colours, and the placement of lucky pieces.

The Feng Shui expert usually goes to the scene to give advice. The cost can be very high; a scandal in Hong Kong involved the expenditure of a million dollars of public money on the Feng Shui man for a science institute.

It is normal in Hong Kong for Feng Shui to be taken into account at the planning stage. Most developers place high importance on Feng Shui and architects and designers consult and work with Feng Shui masters.

Some common Feng Shui beliefs

A good house should face the sea with its back to a mountain, *buee sarn meen hoy*, 背山面海, back mountain face sea. The water (sea, lake or river) represents wealth coming into the house, and the mountain behind supports the occupant; it also stops the wealth from going out the back door.

A house facing a rough mountainside is not good. The bumpy slope is not only unpleasant to the eye, it is also believed to bring bad health.

A house facing a cemetery is considered an unpleasant view to most Chinese. To those involved in illegal activities, however, it is good luck.

A house near a temple or a church turns women into widows.

A river running right in front of the house is bad luck. The water becomes a blade to hurt the residents. In modern cities, a busy flyover is considered a variation of a river. Particularly when the flyover is situated at the bottom of the high rise, it is said to "cut the legs" of the residents.

A roof beam above the bed is bad for your health.

In the layout of a house, no two doors should face each other directly. This creates "killing air", *sart hay*, 殺氣, thus bringing bad luck. To solve the problem, put a cupboard or screen between the doors.

Hanging Aeolian bells near windows can also reduce "killing air".

This "killing air" is actually a through draught, considered unhealthy. When Aeolian bells ring in the draught it is thought to indicate the presence of evil spirits and is a signal to close windows or doors.

Goldfish or carp are pets that change luck. In dark corners of a house or office, red goldfish are kept to bring in good luck and chase away bad luck. A fish pond in the garden serves the same purpose. In very bright corners, black goldfish are kept to absorb the bad luck.

Moving water changes luck. Indoor fountains, etc., are popular as water represents wealth; running water implies continuous generation of wealth, very important to businessmen and investors.

Leafy plants, such as bamboo or palm trees, indicate growth and can also enhance wealth and bring good luck They are usually placed in the bad luck corner (as advised by the Feng Shui master).

Red carpets and red door mats bring good luck and enhance good fortune.

A mirror placed on top of a windowsill or roof beam to reflect light (which is bad luck) sends the bad luck to one's neighbours. This is a desperate step, as hurting the luck of others will in itself attract bad karma.

Solving problems

Any life trauma or question can be referred to a fortune teller for help. It is also common to seek help from the Gods in various temples: *kow cheem*, 求籤, ask the bamboo stick.

Participants pick up a container of bamboo sticks numbered from one to 100. Some temples may have a few more or less than 100 sticks. They give the presiding God information about themselves, generally just introducing themselves by name in a soft voice. The presiding God is determined by the statue in front of which the prayer is made.

The problem is then outlined. Common questions involve examination results, buying property, marriage, health, lawsuits, long journeys, horse racing, and Mark Six. The container is shaken until one stick drops out.

Each problem presented requires the petitioner to start the procedure from the beginning. In Mark Six, for instance, six or more shakes of the container are required.

From the number on the stick, the participant looks up a temple note with the corresponding number. Each temple has its own set of notes and you can go from temple to temple and get completely different readings from the same number, or the same reading from different numbers. Generally, there are 35% good luck readings, 46% so-so readings, and 19% bad luck readings.

The notes are yours to take away once you have paid the fee – generally nominal, a few dollars only.

Each note states whether it is good or bad luck and the story or myth recounted is in the form of a poem about historical and legendary characters, *gwoo yun*, 古人.

A fortune teller is usually asked to interpret the notes or to suggest a solution. The fortune teller might advise that a set of papers be purchased to be burnt for good luck, *jok fook*, 作福, make fortune. Also *gwye yun*, 貴人, honourable person, paper representational champions, might be purchased where intercession is needed.

Interpreting a Chinese Character, *Chark Jee,* 測字

This is another way in which fortune tellers solve problems. The petitioner writes down a Chinese character and then asks the fortune teller to answer a question. The fortune teller interprets the meaning and structure of the character to solve the problem.

For example, the petitioner writes *yun* 仁 and asks the fortune teller if he should do business with Mr Chan. The fortune teller may say, 仁 means benevolence, it is formed by the characters for "people" and "two," yes, the two of you form a good business partnership. Or he may say, it is formed by "people" and "two," 二 is formed by two parallel lines, there is no point of contact, the two of you will not reach agreement on business matters. The solution very much depends on the insight of the fortune teller.

Naming a Child or Person

Fortune tellers are consulted in the naming of children, generally so that the life of the parents can be improved by choosing a propitious name. This is not entirely selfish. The hope implied by the name for a bright future or a steady and healthy life for the child only incidentally rubs off on the parents as it must therefore mean that they are living well. This is very much part of the Chinese sense of family and the thought that each member owes a duty to all other members of the family and that this duty extends to physical well-being.

By providing the precise time of birth the fortune teller knows which of the five elements the child belongs to. The elements are metal, wood, water, fire, and earth, *gum, mook, soy, for, to,* 金, 木, 水, 火, 土. Even if the fortune teller does not specify the exact name or character to be used for the best chances of success in life, parents might choose one from a list provided or because the character contains representations of the element which the fortune teller says is missing from the balance.

> Wong Yum Meew, 王鑫淼. It is clear from the characters of his name that this son of the Wong family was found to have both metal (金) and water (水) missing from his balance for a good life.
>
> Similarly, it would seem from Yip Mook Sum, 葉木森, that Mr Yip was missing wood (木) for good balance.

Another method of choosing a name might be based on the number of strokes which make up the characters of the name, thus providing a numerical balance when taken with time of birth and other factors.

> Betty Hung's Chinese name is Huung Bik Yee, 孔碧儀. Counting the strokes in the characters gives 4 + 14 + 15, a total of 33 which is a very lucky number. But if you render that name in its simplified form, 孔碧仪, the strokes are 4 + 14 + 5, for a total of 23. The question then arises of whether, if she moved to Singapore where simplified characters are used, Hung would have a different fate.

As a last-ditch attempt to change your luck, fortune tellers might advise a name change. As with naming children, the selection of a new name might be based on achieving balance through addition of one or more of the five elements or the number of strokes.

> Actors, actresses, singers and others in the entertainment field need an "artist name," ngye meng, 藝名. This name should be unique, easy to remember and auspicious. Fewer strokes in the surname is preferable because the Chinese method of "alphabeticising" is to put the characters with fewer strokes first.

Changing or selecting friends and clothes

Even these most personal aspects of life are not immune to the sway of the fortune teller. The calculations used are based on the five elements.

Taking again Betty Hung's Chinese name as an example, the fortune teller might say that she abounds in wood but lacks fire. To balance this lack she should wear warm (fiery) colours and earth tones in order to nurture and strengthen the wood element which is essential to her nature.

When choosing a partner (business or social, with a view to permanency or not) she will be best served by partners with a strong metal element in their make-up. This is because metal is used to shape wood into something useful.

She should avoid partnerships with persons with strong fire or wood elements as these people might hurt her. On the contrary, those with strong water or earth can only help her to grow stronger, but she must take care around them lest their influence cause her to grow in weight and size rather than in goodness and success!

20

Number Superstitions

Lucky numbers

2, *yee*, 二, easy. Sounds like *yee,* 易, easy.

8, *bart*, 八, get wealth. Sounds like *fart*, 發, prosperity. It is used in such lucky phrases as *fart choy*, 發財, make money and *fart dart*, 發達, be prosperous.

> Developers make it a selling point if an address includes the number eight. Instead of giving the building a lucky name they might just use the address.

9, *gow*, 九, eternal. Sounds like *gow*, 久, from the phrase *cherng gow*, 長久, long lasting, forever.

18, *sup bart*, 十八, prosperity. Sounds like *sut fart*, 實發, sure to make money and be prosperous.

28, *yee bart*, 二八, easy pickings. Sounds like *yee fart*, 易發, easy to make money.

138, *yut sarm bart*, 一三八, lifelong financial ease. Sounds like *yut sung fart*, 一生發, make money and be prosperous your whole life.

338, *sarm sarm bart,* 三三八, eternal financial ease. Sounds like *sung sung fart,* 生生發, make money and be prosperous now and in future reincarnations.

668, *look look bart,* 六六八, prosper in all fields of endeavour. Sounds like *lo lo fart,* 路路發, you will make money and be prosperous on life's journey. An especially good choice for a vehicle licence plate.

1168, *yut yut look bart,* 一一六八, increase your wealth. Sounds like *yut yut look jook fart,* 日日陸續發, continue making money every day.

1314, *yut sarm yut say,* 一三一四, throughout life. Sounds like *yut sung yut sye,* 一生一世, the whole life. Often used in lovers' declarations and wedding ceremonies.

Taboo numbers

4, *say,* 四, death. Sounds like *say,* 死, death.

13, *sup sarm,* 十三, only unlucky when it applies to the 13th floor, the superstition has crossed over from Western influence. In Cantonese it is a lucky sound, as *sut sung,* 實生, certainly survive.

14, *sup say,* 十四, inevitable death. Sounds like *sut say,* 實死, certainly must die.

24, *yee say,* 二四, death comes easily. Sounds like *yee say,* 易死, easy to die.

5, *ng/mm,* 五, negative, no. Sounds like *mm,* 唔, no, not.

58, *mm bart,* 五八, bad financial management. Sounds like *mm fart,* 唔 發, not making money and not prosperous.

Many buildings in Hong Kong do not have a 4th, 14th, or 24th floor. Some lack a 13th floor as well. Property developers worry such "unlucky" real estate will not find a ready market. It is not unknown for developers to wrongly claim a building has 88 floors when in reality there are only 80.

1358, *yut sarm mm bart*, 一三五八, lifetime of poverty. Sounds like *yut sung mm fart*, 一生唔發, a whole life not making money.

5354, *mm sarm mm say*, 五三五四, good for nothing. Sounds like *mm sarm mm say*, 唔三唔四, cannot achieve anything, fit for nothing. Of a woman, indecent, promiscuous. Also sounds like *mm sarng mm say*, 唔生唔死, neither alive nor dead.

7, *chut*, 七, a) funeral. The number seven is used in Chinese funerals. b) Penis. Sounds like *chut* (no character), a profanity for the male sex organ.

9, *gow*, 九, penis. Sounds like *gow* (閪), a profanity for penis.

9413, *gow say yut sarm*, 九四一三, tempting fate, high likelihood of death. Sounds like *gow say yut sang*, 九死一生, a narrow escape from death, literally 90% dead 10% alive.

Interesting Cantonese phrases concerning numbers

Lum ba wun, 冧巴溫, is a sound-alike for the English 'number one'. The Chinese Almanac has a chapter which teaches English through the use of Chinese characters on the "sounds-like" principle.

Yut gor, 一哥, brother number one. Refers to the leading man in a business, and also the head of police, because he has car licence plate number one.

Yut jair, 一姐, sister number one. Refers to the leading woman in a business.

A yut, 阿一, number one. Sir/Madam.

A yee, 阿二, number two. Number two wife, mistress.

Yee nye, 二奶, two wife. Number two wife, mistress. Prior to 1971 concubinage was legal in Hong Kong and no shame was attached to the position of number two (or three, etc.) wife.

Yee nye jye, 二奶仔, two wife boy. A man, a department, or a thing which is unprofitable or not of particular importance. Generally used reflexively by someone who feels hard-done-by, overlooked.

Yee mm jye, 二五仔, two five boy. Traitor, a betrayer.

Yee da look, 二打六, two hit six. Bit part players in movies or drama.

Yee bart teen, 二八天, two eight weather. Refers to the short period between winter and summer in Hong Kong. The change is not obvious, lasting less than a month.

Sarm sum lerng yee, 三心兩意, three hearts two minds. Indecision.

Up sarm up say, 噏三噏四, talk three talk four. Gossip, particularly maliciously and irresponsibly.

Sarm (gow) mm sik chut, 三(九)唔識七, three (and nine) do not know seven. An expression of unease if circumstances dictate proximity with a complete stranger.

A say, 阿四, number four child. Derogatory nickname for gofers. In the past, the parents of Chinese domestic helpers were seldom educated, so they named their children numerically. *A Say* was a common name for helpers.

Say jye, 四仔, four boy, slang for a category IV pornographic DVD.

Say tuung bart dart, 四通八達, can reach every direction. Very accessible to public and private transport. The phrase has been adopted to mean Octopus Card: *bart dart tuung*, 八達通. The Hong Kong Octopus Card is a prepaid cash card used on public transport as well as for general purchases.

Mm mm bor, 五五波, five five chance. Your chances are 50/50.

Mm ngarn look sik, 五顏六色, five and six colours. Very colourful.

Mm see fa look see been, 五時花六時變, a flower at five o'clock will have changed by six o'clock. Said of a person, particularly a girl, who often changes her mind.

Lewn chut bart jo, 亂七八糟, seven and eight mess. Chaotic, in a mess, in a muddle.

Chut serng bart lok, 七上八落, seven up eight down. Perturbed or uneasy.

Bart por, 八婆, eight woman. A nosy woman, a gossip.

Gow mm darp bart, 九唔搭八, nine is not connected to eight. The answer is not related to the matter concerned. Used of someone who speaks and acts in a brainless manner.

Gow sing gow, 九成九, 99%. A very high possibility.

Sup sing sup, 十成十, 100%. Definitely, certainly, no other possibility.

Sup sarm deem, 十三點, 13 o'clock. A fussy girl.

Sup mm sup look, 十五十六, 15 and 16. Cannot make up one's mind.

21

Good Luck and Bad Luck

Dressing for good luck

When going to the races or gambling, both men and women wear red underwear for luck, sometimes with a double happiness symbol embroidered or printed on the fabric. Piggy underpants are also a great favourite.

Gold is another lucky colour, but not so popular as red, because it is reflective and draws too much attention to the wearer. Often the metallic threads are uncomfortable to wear – particularly in underwear.

Changing your luck

The Chinese way of dealing with a run of bad luck, at the mahjong table for instance, is to move the angle of the light, wash their hands, or make a noise by pulling the drawers in and out, before resuming play.

In extreme circumstances, both men and women might take off their lucky red underwear and wave it around the room to chase away the bad luck before resuming gambling.

Surgical excision of blemishes also removes the associated bad luck. Moles on the back mean unremitting hard work. A pair of moles on a woman's cheeks either side of the nose signify that she will be widowed. Cosmetic surgery in Chinese women is more often a matter of protecting her loved ones (or giving herself a chance to marry) than mere vanity. A more prominent nose and cheek is seen as bringing good luck to a husband and this surgery is treated as an investment in the security of the marriage.

Changing your given name to change your luck is a last-ditch attempt advised by fortune tellers. The new name might be based on the total number of strokes in the characters which go to make up the name, or it might be based on the meanings of the elements of the characters. The fortune teller might advise, for instance, that more fire is needed and the new name will include words using fire elements.

> **Someone who lacks fire (火) or wood (木) in his life may be told to use 燊 or 榮 in his name.**

Changing or selecting friends is often based on similar calculations. Again, this is usually on the advice of fortune tellers. Naming one's offspring follows similar lines so that your life can be improved by choosing a propitious name for your baby.

Lucky charms

Pendants or bracelets blessed by Buddhist monks in a special ceremony, *Hoy Gwong*, 開光, reveal divine wisdom, are used as amulets. These are usually jade, semi-precious stones, crystal, or gold and might be sent as gifts to impart the blessings to a loved one. They can be bought from souvenir stalls in temples.

Bad luck meetings

Generally meeting a bald-headed person is considered bad luck when going gambling. A shiny bald head is seen as irritating to the eyes and might attract ill fortune.

Though Chinese seek protection from Buddha, meeting Buddhist nuns and monks is considered bad luck because the shaved head indicates emptiness. Ancient Chinese social hierarchy placed monks and nuns at the bottom of the pecking order, just one step above beggars.

Good luck and bad luck animals

A black cat is considered bad luck, especially if unexpectedly sighted. No bad luck attaches to keeping a black cat as a pet.

A crow brings bad luck with it.

Hay jerk, 喜鵲, magpies are good luck birds, particularly near the house in the morning. They presage happiness, especially forthcoming nuptials. The characters sound like happiness and jumping up and down with joy.

Putting your arm around another's shoulders

Just don't. This is extremely offensive to Chinese because of the belief that the soul is characterised by lights which shine on each shoulder. These protective lights are visible only to ghosts and are obscured for the rest of the day if you put your arm around another's shoulders. The person then appears to ghosts to be dead. The lights reignite the next day but while they are out the person risks being able to see ghosts, other unlighted beings, a most undesirable condition.

The area across the top of the shoulders is considered the main depository of good luck, especially as related to wealth, and to have another interfere in this area causes misfortune.

The gesture, so casual and friendly in Western culture, elicits strong reactions, even real terror among Chinese. It is never considered friendly or funny.

22

Auspicious Foods

Hong Kong Chinese have various superstitions about food. Some of the more common foods served at dinner parties or as offerings to the gods are:

Gye, 雞, whole chicken, represents the mythical Phoenix which in turn represents the Empress, an offering to the Gods.

Seeu yook, 燒肉, roast pork, an offering to the Gods.

Fay jew yook, 肥豬肉, fatty pork, an offering to the Gods (and demons). The oiliness of the pork is believed to glue the mouths of the demons shut so that they cannot spread their evil lies.

Yew jew, 乳豬, roast suckling pig, an offering to the gods, a symbol of virginity in a bride.

Ha, 蝦, prawns, laughter, *ha ha dye seeu,* 哈哈大笑, a big laugh. The sound, *ha,* is like laughter. Prawns curl up when cooked, and look like laughing eyes.

Luung ha, 龍蝦, lobster, literally, dragon prawn. Laughter.

Yew, 魚, whole fish, sounds like surplus, *neen neen yow yew,* 年年有餘, a surplus every year, a good wish for Chinese New Year.

Sarng yew, 生魚, live fish, full of vitality.

Lay yew, 鯉魚, carp, the fish fairy in Chinese mythology. It leaped ten thousand times to get through the dragon gate into heaven, *lay yerk luung moon,* 鯉躍龍門.

Bow yew, 鮑魚, abalone, guaranteed surplus.

Yew chee, 魚翅, shark's fin, sounds like eagles spreading their wings to fly away, *dye parng jeen chee,* 大鵬展翅.

Fart choy, 髮菜, sea moss, sounds like *fart choy,* 發財, making money.

Ho see, 蠔士, dried oyster, sounds like good business, *ho see,* 好市.

Jew lay, 豬脷, pork tongue, sounds like *dye lay,* 大利, huge profit.

Jew sow, 豬手, pork knuckle, sounds like money comes easily to hand, *sarng choy jow sow,* 生財就手.

Sarng choy, 生菜, lettuce, sounds like make money, *sarng choy,* 生財.

Duung gwu, 冬菇, Chinese dried mushroom, looks like ancient money, gold nuggets.

Leen ngow, 蓮藕, lotus root, sounds like find a true love, *gye ngow teen sing,* 佳偶天成. Also, because there are many holes in the lotus root, it means access all areas, *lo lo serng tuung,* 路路相通, a requirement of good business.

Chuung, 葱, spring onion, sounds like smart and clever, *chuung ming,* 聰明.

Kun choy, 芹菜, Chinese celery, sounds like work hard, be industrious, *kun lik,* 勤力.

Huung lor bark, 紅蘿蔔, carrot, favourite food of rabbits, a symbol of cleverness. The orange, reddish colour is auspicious.

Lye see choy, 利是菜, lucky bunch of vegetables. These include celery, lettuce, carrot, and spring onion. The bunch is first offered to the Gods and then used in dishes to bring good luck to the family and make children smarter.

Charng, 橙, orange, the colour is similar to gold. The most common offering to the Gods, the round shape symbolises wholeness, completion. When a child gives a sour orange to his grandparents, they eat it and say: it is sour, *ho sewn,* 好酸, which sounds the same as good grandchild, *ho sewn,* 好孫.

Fa sung, 花生, peanuts, also called the nut with many seeds, *dor jye gwor,* 多仔果, because there is always more than one nut per pod and they grow in clusters. It is a symbol of having many children.

To, 桃, peach, a symbol of longevity. In Chinese mythology, the peach tree grown in heaven takes three thousand years to blossom, three thousand years to bear fruit, and another three thousand years for the fruit to ripen, a total of nine thousand years to produce each peach. These long-awaited peaches are then presented to the emperor's mother in the court of heaven as a birthday present.

Cherng jye serng darn, 腸仔雙蛋, one sausage and two eggs. On the morning of an examination, it is good luck to eat a sausage with two fried eggs, because it looks like 100 on the plate.

Inauspicious foods

Mooi choy, 梅菜, pickled plum leaf, sounds like bad luck, not prosperous, *mooi,* 霉, mildew. The leaves look like un-ironed clothes, implying someone is not properly dressed.

Harm yew, 鹹魚, salted fish, stiff and smelly, like a dead body.

Duung gwa dow foo, 冬瓜豆腐, winter melon and tofu, soft foods, like a dead body, without strength.

Bark gwor, 白果, ginkgo, sounds like a nil result, something done in vain.

Jeeu, 蕉, banana, sounds like failure, scorched, burnt. If you want to tell someone to go to hell, the euphemism is: "go eat a banana," *sik jeeu la,* 食蕉啦. It is also a euphemism for oral sex.

Ling muung, 檸檬, lemon, the Cantonese saying, *sik ling muung,* 食檸檬, eat a lemon, means a man is upset because a girl he asked to dance turned him down.

Yut look got, 一碌葛, kudzu, (a tuberous vegetable used in Chinese cooking), a man who is not so bright.

PART VI

MATTERS MEDICAL

23

CHINESE DOCTORS

Chinese doctors

You hear about acupuncturists, herbal doctors, bone setters, and so on. All are based on a single philosophy and these are just specialities, like O&G or ENT in Western medicine. In Hong Kong, all practitioners of both Chinese and Western medicine must be licensed and registered to practise.

Juung yee, 中醫, herbal doctor

Chinese believe that when the natural balance of the body is upset, people fall ill. The two main approaches to restoring balance are strengthening the immune system and creating undesirable conditions for the problem to continue.

During the SARS epidemic of 2003, the second approach was taken. The populace was encouraged to improve their general health by eating herbs and paying special attention to hygiene. The herbs prescribed were aimed at creating an atmosphere not conducive to the growth of the virus, rather than attacking it, so that the body's own mechanisms were able to deal with the problem naturally. An attractive aspect of this approach is minimisation of side effects from drugs.

To assess a problem, Chinese herbal doctors go through the process of *mong mun mun cheet,* 望聞問切, look listen ask diagnose.

'Look' includes the patient's general aspect as well as taking both primary and secondary pulses and life signs, *ba muck,* 把脈. Next, the doctor listens to the patient describe his problem and then asks questions to clarify before making a diagnosis.

十問歌 The 10 inquiries song
明代張景岳 from Zhang Jing Yue of the Ming Dynasty
一問寒熱二問汗 三問頭身四問便 五問飲食六問
胸 七聾八渴俱當辨 九問舊病十問因 再問服藥
參機變 女問經產兒問痘疹

I ask cold hot 2 ask sweat 3 ask head body 4 ask excrement
5 ask diet 6 ask chest 7 deaf 8 thirst should all be identified
9 old illness 10 reason then ask what medicine was taken
to consider any change women ask menstruation and
birth children ask smallpox measles/rash

Herbs are then prescribed. Some are to heal, and some to neutralize adverse side effects of the healing herb. *Boon Cho Gong Muuk,* 本草綱目, a famous book from the Sung Dynasty listing the properties and uses of herbs, is still used today. It has been amended over the years and is the herbal doctors' bible.

Some herbal doctors work out of their own offices, and many more work from desks in herb shops. Many herb shops

offer a service to concoct the potion. This can be a very smelly process.

Jum gow, 針灸, acupuncture

The use of long, fine needles to stimulate the body so that it will regulate itself. Western medical studies have shown that acupuncture points are in fact the junctures of nerves and the effect is like receiving a low current electric shock.

Acupuncture enjoys a reputation as being very effective in dealing with chronic pain, muscle repair, stopping smoking, and even growing hair. Acupuncturists work out of their own offices.

Tit da, 跌打, bonesetter

Target problems are muscular aches and pains and broken bones. You will not leave a bonesetter without being given a poultice to soothe the pain which is left in place for 12 to 24 hours. The main effective ingredient used to be tiger bones but this is now banned and the substitutes are not thought to be as effective.

Bonesetters work out of clinics and little privacy is afforded to the patient. The discipline is learned though an apprenticeship as well as formal study.

Fook wye, 復位, chiropractor

Much like in Western medicine, Chinese chiropractors deal with the re-alignment of the spine through manipulation. They work out of their own offices.

Hay guung, 氣功, qigong

This can be practised by oneself as routine exercise. A master is able to use his Qi (energy) to heal another through massage. It is generally used for pain control and to regulate the minor imbalances. A Qigong master works out of his own offices.

Toy na, 推拿, massage

Massage is an enormously popular indulgence in Hong Kong for the relief of pain and muscle fatigue.

Foot reflexology is a derivative form of massage, believed to increase metabolism and maintain health. The foot is seen as a map of the human body. Massage of the toes cures problems with the head, including insomnia; the digestive system can be improved by massage of the arch, etc.

But gwoon, 拔罐, the use of vacuum glass cups. The cups are applied to the back or shoulder and left until the skin is marked. No pain is involved. Some people bruise quite badly, in others just a faint mark is visible. It represents the toxins leaving the body.

Gwart sa, 刮痧, the use of a tool with a smooth edge, e.g. a HK$1 coin, to rub the neck, shoulders, ribs and back until the area is bruised in stripes. No pain is involved even though it can look quite dramatic. The breaking down of the capillaries is believed to increase metabolism and heal muscular pain and flu.

Massage parlours are thick on the street in Hong Kong. Most take walk-in business; you may need to book at the more popular times or for the more popular practitioners.

The massage parlours are licensed and it is up to the licensee to hire trained professionals, each of whom must be registered with the appropriate government body.

24

Medical Superstitions

Obsessive head protection

Chinese find the Western habit of wearing hats and carrying umbrellas against rain a little odd. Hats are seen as a fashion statement rather than a protective covering against sun or rain. There is little skin cancer in the Chinese community, or if there is it is not common knowledge, and this is not part of the thought process.

Chinese tend to keep umbrellas at work and home. If caught short they buy one as the need arises. It is not normal practice to take an umbrella if the weather man says rain threatens, probably because the predictions are often wrong and very inexact as to both the area to be affected and the time the rain is expected.

When no umbrella is to hand, Chinese have a habit of putting a hand flat over the top of the head as if it were a mini-umbrella. Even lifeguards, dressed for swimming, will be seen frantically running for shelter with a hand over their head at the first sign of rain. Men and women of all ages can be seen with a single disposable tissue placed on top of their heads as some sort of protection from a downpour.

From birth, Chinese parents drum into their offspring the urban myth of *tow fuung*, 頭風, head wind, supposedly the cause of headaches in the elderly. They rationalise that getting your head wet leads to sickness, and, as you age, results in frequent headaches.

This extends to new mothers who are prohibited by custom from washing their hair for a full calendar month after giving birth (see Pregnancy, below).

Other areas carefully kept dry and warm are the nape of the neck, the sole of the foot, the lower back, and the lower abdominal region. The lengths to which Chinese go to protect these areas can be quite humorous to outsiders. Children at play, for instance, often have thick towels stuffed down their T-shirts to absorb perspiration – whatever the weather.

Sunshine phobia

Chinese do not traditionally wear hats yet go to extraordinary lengths to protect themselves from direct sunlight. You will not see Chinese sitting at tables outside restaurants, no matter how balmy the weather, if there is any alternative. Should they find themselves seated (inside or out) so that the sun shines on them, chairs are moved into the shade; fellow diners seem to understand and make space rather than be angry that their area is being diminished.

UV-cutting umbrellas are a hot sale item in Hong Kong. Young children are avidly protected from the sun's rays. The availability of SPF 40+ products is a result of this phobia, as is the high price in the region for such products.

Fair skin is taken as a mark of beauty. It used to be a mark of the upper classes, and to obtain it not only is direct sunlight avoided but skin whitening products are freely used.

Yut bark jair sarm chow, 一白遮三醜, one white covers three ugliness. This common expression explains the lengths to which Chinese go to stay fair.

Bed socks

Use of bed socks is forbidden. It is believed this pampering will break down the body's natural resistance and in some way slow down circulation.

The ground's negative energy

Touching the ground with one's bare flesh is a no-no. The local belief is that the ground exudes some sort of negative energy which will be absorbed by direct contact.

Going barefooted, therefore, or either lying or sleeping on the ground, is taboo. When picnicking or sunbathing, Chinese always take a groundsheet to ward off any bad luck the ground may otherwise impart. The groundsheet need not be substantial.

Medically, ground chill is believed to lead to rheumatism in later life.

Waiting for the seat to cool down

Cantonese find it unpleasant and feel it unhygienic to take a seat still warm with the previous occupant's body heat.

Either they stand guard in front of the seat or sit perched on the very edge until the seat has cooled down. The urban myth is that absorbing another's body heat causes haemorrhoids (piles).

Facing the horses

When taking a bus or train, Chinese do not like to sit with their backs to the driver. It is believed to induce dizziness.

Drinking hot water

Chinese like to drink hot, not iced, water. All drinks are preferred hot and this might be based on Chinese herbal doctors' contention that, by keeping the liquids at the same temperature as the body (38°C), no physical reaction ensues.

Cold drinks are thought to have a deleterious effect on the body which can start a chain reaction leading to ill health.

Ice, in particular, is seen as something which inhibits the proper function of the waste elimination processes and, therefore, exposes the ice-eater to a tendency to gain weight. This is explained by saying that ingestion of ice and cold drinks slows down the metabolism so that the whole detoxifying system, liver, kidneys, lymph, etc., is inhibited in its function. By not efficiently eliminating waste, it is believed to remain in the body, causing weight gain.

Pregnancy

Not all Chinese superstitions about pregnancy are peculiar to the Chinese. Some are universal; some are shared by some cultures but not others. Here, we have taken a broad sample of old wives' tales and folklore and you might find that "modern" medicine in your area has either caught up with or bypassed some of the recommendations. None of them is meant to be taken as advice, it is merely recounted as a matter of interest.

Taboos: Traditional advice is that the couple do not announce the pregnancy until three months. The secret is best kept between the couple, not even close family being let in on the happy news. Folklore says that the baby is very narrow minded, will be angered by any talk about it, and that this anger might cause miscarriage.

Cold food is said to cause miscarriage. Therefore, ice cream, watermelon, cold drinks, etc., are proscribed, even during extremely hot weather.

For the entire pregnancy, the woman should not hammer a nail. It is believed that this causes physical damage to the baby, such as dimples.

Similarly, a pregnant woman should not put stickers or posters on the wall, lest the sticker leave a birthmark on the baby.

The woman should not put a pole through a hole. Village mosquito nets are set up with a bamboo pole through an eyelet in the net. This action could pierce a hole under the nose, causing a harelip.

During pregnancy, it is strictly forbidden to move house, particularly to demolish the marriage bed. Even though the pregnant woman is not personally involved in any of the work of moving, the move itself will affect the baby and cause miscarriage.

Pregnant women should always cover the neck, shoulders, and stomach; she should avoid windy or cool places, and must not catch a cold, lest it affect the baby.

Swimming is believed to cause miscarriage, as is soaking in the bath or any immersion in water.

Stretching the hands up high is said to cause premature birth or miscarriage.

Pregnant women are not strictly forbidden to climb up and down or to do heavy work. As a member of a class, however, a pregnant woman is the most protected creature on Earth. Not only family, but complete strangers, go out of their way to offer any assistance they see she might require – often assistance that she does not want until the very care becomes a burden.

Treatment during pregnancy: A herbal tea called *sup sarm tye bo,* 十三太保, is taken to secure the foetus in the womb.

To overcome morning sickness, sour food is advised. Examples are pickled ginger, pickled lemon and dried sour plum, *wa muee,* 話梅.

This has led to a belief that all pregnant women love sour food, so when a young woman suddenly becomes fond of sour food, she is suspected to be pregnant.

Just before birth: Just before going to hospital to give birth, women shower and shampoo. After giving birth, they are not supposed to touch "raw" water for a month.

There are various reasons and explanations given for this. Water may be unclean, it contains negative energy, water is thought to cause rheumatic aches called wind, *fuung*, 風, in the bones which affects the health of the woman, and causes future headaches and rheumatic problems.

After giving birth: To release the wind, *fuung*, caused by labour, ginger is the new mother's best friend. This should be eaten with fried rice.

She is advised not to shower, and especially not to shampoo her hair. If she feels she must, then she should use water boiled with ginger peel. Traditional wisdom dictates that she should do no more than take a sponge bath using ginger peel water for a full month after birth.

New mothers take nourishing tonics and special foods to regain their strength. Sweet vinegar with ginger, eggs and pork knuckle is the most popular foodstuff – it is made in quantity as a gift to spread the good news to family and friends. Eggs are cheap but provide energy. Pork knuckle is rich in collagen, which, dissolved in the vinegar, is easy for the mother to absorb. Northern Chinese eat fried sesame seeds for the same reasons.

A sort of Karatane Nurse, a *Pooi Yewt*, 陪月, is employed to take care of the mother and child for the first month or up to 100 days after birth. She usually lives in.

The first month after giving birth is known as *chor yewt*, 坐月, (literally, sit month) and is a serious matter in the family. All new mothers are believed to be weak and are expected to do nothing but rest in the first month.

The *pooi yewt* is a specialist (a training course is offered at Hong Kong's Labour Retraining Council, *Goo Yewn Joy Pooi Fun Gook*, 僱員再培訓局) who knows all the dos and don'ts for the new mother. She prepares the mother's food and guides her in the care of the baby.

Using a *puee yut* is also said to reduce the chance of post-natal depression.

Breastfeeding is popular in China. Green papaya and fish soup are said to increase the milk flow.

Powdered milk is said to cause the baby to suffer from "heatiness," *yeet hay*, 熱氣, resulting in constipation and poor sleep. If using formula, herbs called make milk tea, *hoy nye cha*, 開奶茶, available at herbal stores, are used to prepare the liquid part of the formula.

Sex for the couple is forbidden during pregnancy and after birth for 100 days up to one year.

Menstruation

Anti-stress foods such as rose or chrysanthemum tea, and Chinese wolfberry, *gow gay jee*, 枸杞子, in soup are advised just prior to menstruation.

Hot food (see chapter 25) is said to delay onset, while cold food might cause early onset and increased flow as well as more severe cramps. Cold food is forbidden during menstruation.

Red dates, *huung jo,* 紅棗, and Chinese herbs like Chinese angelica, *dong gye,* 當歸, and pseudo-ginseng, *teen chut,* 田七, are considered good choices to regenerate blood after menstruation and generally replenish the woman's health.

Menopause

Chinese doctors hold that strengthening the functions of the liver and spleen will relieve problems of see-sawing emotions and help to overcome poor sleep patterns which might develop at this time. If all the organs are functioning well, symptoms such as hot flushes and night sweats are taken as part of life and not problems requiring treatment.

25

FOOD AS MEDICINE

This subject is too large for more than a very brief overview here. Many detailed studies of the topic are available for those wishing to delve further into this arcane area of nutrition.

Chinese categorise body type into either *yeet,* 熱, hot or *hon lerng,* 寒涼, cold. This does not mean hot of temperature, the classifications might as well be round or square. Symptoms of a hot body include bad breath, pimples, sore throat, and a preference for cold drinks; symptoms of a cold body include dizzy spells and a preference for hot drinks. Both one's body type and the prevailing weather are considered when selecting what to eat or drink.

Food is categorised into a seemingly unlimited number of types under general headings such as hot, mild, cool, cold, organ specific, detoxifying, nourishing, etc.

Although they may not know why, most Chinese can tell what foods fall into which category, and what effects they will have on the body.

From earliest childhood, the principles of balancing diet in order to treat minor ailments are drummed into the Chinese, not only by older family members but also by waiters, friends and acquaintances. Food marketers take advantage of this cultural obsession by making claims of health benefits, often wildly optimistic, for their products.

In Hong Kong, food is the most prevalent topic of conversation, be it where or what to eat, or, more often, why to eat which food in order to cure what ailment. One result: no privacy for your minor ailments. A waiter is quite likely to say, "Oh, eat this, it's good for getting rid of pimples."

Beliefs about particular foods are not China-wide. The Shanghainese believe bamboo shoots are a cure-all, for instance, while Cantonese see them as toxic.

Yeet hay, 熱氣, *cho yeet,* 燥熱, or simply *cho,* 燥, hot, is probably the most commonly discussed food category. Eating foods in this category worsens the situation if the patient has a sore throat, pimples or boils, bad temper, halitosis, insomnia, constipation, etc.

Hot foods include all fried and roast foods as well as all baked goods, coffee, highly spiced dishes, MSG (*may jing,* 味精), chocolate, lychees and durian.

Hot foods are also contra-indicated for pregnant women (pregnant women fall into the hot category whatever their normal body type) who should also avoid cold foods, said to cause miscarriage.

Ching yeet, 清熱, *ha for,* 下火, fire quenching. This grouping is the "cure" for hot body types to seek balance. Examples are vegetable soup, salty food, and beer (*bair jow,* 啤酒, known locally as *gwye lo lerng cha,* 鬼佬涼茶, herbal tea for foreigners).

Hon lerng, 寒涼, cold, is believed to adversely affect mental stability and to cause poor circulation. The group is thought to increase the unpleasant symptoms of menstruation including cramping and to dramatically increase flow.

Cold foods include salad, watermelon, green tea, and pak choi.

Sup dook, 濕毒, humid toxic, believed to lead to allergies, rashes, and constipation. The category includes shrimp, crab, shellfish, and mango. To cure oneself of bodily humidity, eat curry or winter melon soup. To generally detoxify, a tortoise-shell jelly made with herbs is commonly sold and very popular.

Jee yern, 滋潤, nourishing, includes dessert soups, honey, soups made with both fruit and pork or chicken, almonds and ground pearls.

Yee ying bo ying, 以形補形, use shape to supplement shape. General tonics to boost energy, or to target a specific organ, are often based on shape. The part of the animal eaten benefits that part of the diner's body. Brains for brains, lungs for lungs, tendons for strength, etc.

Walnuts are believed to positively affect the brain and the kidneys, and cashew nuts the kidneys. This is because of the "look alike" shape of the nuts. Ginseng, a root which can take the shape of a person, is taken as a general tonic.

Deer antler is taken for blood replenishment. The deer is chased to exhaustion when the blood collects in the antlers, which are then quickly harvested to preserve their blood-engorged state. The deer is not killed. The antlers are sliced into soup which is believed to be of particular benefit to women after menstruation.

Ming mook, 明目, bright eye, vision improvement can be had by drinking chrysanthemum tea.

Neutral foods which can be safely taken at any meal in any weather or health conditions include pork, apples, and choi sum.

At the onset of flu, Cantonese are taught to avoid chicken and to drink herbal tea, available from street stalls, and, nowadays, even convenience stores and supermarkets. Afterwards they go to bed, cover themselves with blankets, and sweat it out.

Some tea sellers enquire after your symptoms and blend a particular concoction to cure what ails you.

Chinese herbal doctors do not recommend these teas, they lie in the category of home remedy but continue to have a wide market.

Food is further divided into five flavours or tastes: sour, bitter, sweet, spicy, and salt. Chinese medical practitioners use the names of the major organs as references for general systems. If told your liver is no good, this does not mean your actual liver. See below.

Sewn, 酸, sour, detoxifies the system and affects the liver, *gon*, 肝. It helps generate saliva, considered important during summer. White vinegar and lemons are sour foods.

Foo, 苦, bitter, balances mental health which is said to rest with the heart, *sum,* 心. Bitter melon and hearts of lotus seed are bitter foods.

Gum, 甘, sweet, eases the digestive system and is nourishing. It affects the spleen, *pay,* 脾. Longan and red dates are sweet foods.

Sun, 辛, spicy, relieves congestion and is good for the lungs, *fye,* 肺. Ginger, spring onions, and garlic are spicy foods.

Harm, 鹹, salt, improves hormonal balance and the lymph system. It affects the kidneys, *sun,* 腎, and is thought to be easily passed from the body because it stimulates the lymph system. It is recommended for those wishing to lose weight. Seaweed is a salt food.

Eating for the weather

In summer, when the weather is hot and humid, certain foods are said to prevent heat stroke. This is known as *hoy sew sup,* 祛暑濕. This group includes melons, green beans, sugar cane, green tea, fresh lotus leaf, watermelon rind and herbs such as *gum ngun fa,* 金銀花, all of which have diuretic properties.

Over-indulgence in water is said to be non-beneficial, causing *sew sup,* 暑濕, which in turn leads to lassitude, loss of appetite, dry mouth, urine retention, nausea, diarrhoea, and even low fever. Food in the "hot" category, oily fried foods, coffee, and alcohol are also proscribed during summer.

In winter, during Hong Kong's cold and dry weather, warm food, *koy hon newn wye,* 驅寒暖胃, is advised for good health. Ginger and lamb fall into this category. Nourishing sweet soups are recommended.

PART VII

DAILY LIFE

26

At the Restaurant

Cleaning cutlery

The first task Cantonese turn to in a Chinese restaurant is sterilising chopsticks, serving spoons, and any other cutlery, in a glass of hot tea. The restaurant provides the tea for drinking, not washing; but it is seldom drunk. Waiters and restaurant proprietors are in no way offended by this obvious distrust of their washing up skills – they would do the same themselves even if they had personally washed the chopsticks earlier in the day. It is simply social custom. Extra tea is ordered for drinking.

In Western restaurants, cutlery is cleaned by wiping it down with a tissue, or the table napkins provided. Locals do not trust the cleanliness of napkins in Chinese restaurants and would not dream of using them to clean either their mouths or their eating tools.

Using the menu

It is not the restaurant which is chosen, it is the type of food. When entering a dining room, Cantonese generally have a good idea of what to order.

Negotiations with the waiter are begun immediately upon being seated. The menu is not relied on, except to see what is discounted, what new ideas the chef has come up with, and whether the signature dish is a good deal.

Restaurants which advertise themselves as *dim sum*, for instance, are expected to offer the standard dishes in the category. Response is likely to be vocal if they cannot be supplied. *Dim sum* menus seldom list price, which is usually on a card on the table and changes depending on the time of day. At non-peak hours, the food is significantly cheaper. The prices are often standardised into three categories: large, *dye,* 大, medium, *juung,* 中, and small, *seeu,* 小.

> More expensive dim sum categories are: *chew,* 廚, *duk,* 特, and *ding,* 頂. As a rule of thumb, the more strokes in the character, the more money changes hands!

If you try to order seven dishes, the waiter will try to sell you one more so as not to tempt fate. Seven is the number of dishes served at funeral banquets. Once you have chosen six dishes, Cantonese waiters are reluctant to take an order for one more dish. They will, however, happily take an order for eight or more dishes.

The most important word in the description of each dish is put at the end. A list of common food names follows.

Farn, 飯, rice.

Meen, 麵, noodles. All types of noodle apart from rice noodles, often egg and/or wheat noodles.

Fun, 粉, rice noodles. Most commonly *mye fun,* 米粉, fine noodles or *hor fun,* 河粉, thick flat noodles.

Tong, 湯, soup.

Gow, 餃, dumpling.

Bow, 包, filled bun.

Yook, 肉, meat, usually pork. Sometimes the full term *jew yook,* 豬肉, pig meat, is used.

Ngow yook, 牛肉, beef.

Yerng yook, 羊肉, lamb or mutton.

Gye, 雞, chicken. To aggrandise an everyday item, chicken might be described as *fuung,* 鳳, phoenix. *Fuung jow,* 鳳爪, phoenix claw, is actually chicken feet.

Ngarp, 鴨, duck.

Ngor, 鵝, goose.

Yew, 魚, fish.

Ha, 蝦, prawn, shrimp.

Hye, 蟹, crab.

Darn, 蛋, egg.

Choy, 菜, vegetable.

Gwa, 瓜, melon.

Dow foo, 豆腐, tofu or bean curd.

Kair jee, 茄子, eggplant or aubergine.

Farn kair, 番茄, tomato (means foreign eggplant).

Chuung, 葱, spring onion.

Yerng chuung, 洋葱, onion (foreign spring onion).

Sewn, 蒜, garlic.

Lart jeeu, 辣椒, chilli, hot peppers.

The word/s preceding the main ingredient might be purely decorative, might refer to the location from which the dish supposedly hails or might be a description of the cooking process. For example, *yerng jow chow farn*, 揚州炒飯, Yangzhou fried rice – the first two characters denote a city in China, the third character is a method of cooking and the final word is rice.

Some locations are now taken as a method of preparation. It can also indicate to those in the know that there has been a price hike.

Food choices

Chinese prefer their fish, fowl, or meat with bones. Removal of chicken or fish skin is not practised as the fat is seen as the most important and flavour-enhancing part of the dish.

The fish fins and head are delicacies, as are chicken feet and the tip of the wing. The chicken breast, on the other hand, is not a favoured part of the bird and is often left on the plate. The thigh of the chicken is the "best" part of the bird and will be offered to the honoured guest, similarly the tail of a fish. Soup is a nourishing food suitable to honour your guest.

Pork knuckle and spare ribs are delicacies, while boneless meat such as rump and fillet steak are chopped up and stewed, or sliced and fried.

Offal: whether flesh, fish, or fowl, is enjoyed. The local perception is that Westerners do not like to eat offal and it will be offered with a big smile and the phrase, "this won't kill you" as an incentive. It usually backfires. Most Westerners are loath to try dishes offered in this way because the smile and the phrase together is generally taken as some sort of trick.

Garnish: the rice paper, fine slice of carrot, or cabbage leaf placed between dim sum and steamer baskets is not eaten – ever. Nor is the leaf which wraps rice dumplings. They are there to stop the food from sticking to the basket and are left on the side of the plate.

By contrast, garnish such as cherries and tinned pineapple are generally eaten.

Cantonese seldom drink the soup served with noodles. The stock is expected to be full of MSG. A separate bowl of soup is ordered if required.

> Q: How come soup is sometimes served at the beginning of the meal, and sometimes at the end?
> A: Sometimes it's served in the middle, too. It depends on the soup and the banquet. Casual meals start with soup, formal banquets serve it in the middle, and soup at the end is sweet, served as a dessert.

Drinking with meals

This is considered bad for one's health. It is said to interfere with the digestive process, much as in some schools of Western thought on diet. Instead of drinking water or tea, Chinese take soup as a substitute.

It is considered bad form to mix rice in your soup and this is also thought to be bad for you. One of the reasons behind this superstition is that you might take the easy way out and just swallow the softened rice without chewing it properly, leading to digestive problems.

Restaurants serve drinks throughout the meal but it is not unusual for Chinese to wait until the meal is almost over before taking liquid, such as dessert soups or tea.

Jew choy, 主菜, the important dish

At Chinese meals, particularly banquets, some dishes are described as *jew choy,* 主菜, often mistranslated as main dish, when what is really meant is that it is expected that the dish will be served. If the dish is omitted, questions are asked. A feeling of discomfort prevails and the omission becomes the subject of gossip for years to come.

Whole chicken and prawns are expected at any banquet. In a Chiu Chow restaurant, goose and sharks' fin are expected among the banquet courses. Peking duck is expected in a Beijing restaurant, etc.

Hong Kong food specialities

Over the years, Hong Kong chefs have delighted in taking ideas from other cuisines and incorporating them into the local diet. This is not so much fusion food as a re-working of classic dishes from other parts of the world, adding, mixing, and substituting ingredients until the original is not recognisable. Often the name is retained unchanged and this presents difficulties if you order Tiramisu, for instance, and are served a pudding where mascarpone has been replaced with custard, amaretto with brandy, sponge finger biscuits with chocolate cake, etc.

Some classic examples of this localising follow.

Sing jow chow mye, 星州炒米, Singapore fried noodles. A very popular dish in Hong Kong but you will not find it in a restaurant in Singapore. You will, however, find Hong Kong fried noodles which is the same dish. This is a bit of tit-for-tat as neither city wishes to lay claim to this rather colonial dish.

The "noodles" part of the description is actually vermicelli rice noodles. Chinese place great importance on the distinction between rice flour noodles, egg noodles, wheat flour noodles, and whether the noodles are flat, round, thin, thick, etc., etc., etc. It is a matter of surprise when Westerners are unconcerned about the type of noodles – they are just noodles.

Pasta oddities. The Cantonese consider pasta part of the noodle family, favouring spaghetti and macaroni. It is believed that Marco Polo introduced noodles and pancakes to the West after his adventures in China. Fast food restaurants, *cha chan teng,*

茶餐廳, have devised many dishes based on pasta made the modern Western way. Some are:

Gon chow hark jeeu ngow yook yee fun, 乾炒黑椒牛肉意粉, fried spaghetti with beef and onions in soy sauce and black pepper. *Gon chow* means that the dish is fried until the sauce blends into the noodles, *hark jeeu,* black pepper, *ngow yook,* beef, *yee fun,* spaghetti.

Herng sewn yook see chow yee, 香蒜肉絲炒意, fried spaghetti with shredded pork and garlic in soy sauce.

Sarm see chow yee, 三絲炒意, fried spaghetti with ham, sausage, BBQ pork and vegetables in soy sauce.

At breakfast, Cantonese like to eat something soupy. Spaghetti in broth with sliced BBQ pork, *cha seeu tong yee,* 叉燒湯意, and macaroni in broth with shredded ham, *for toy tuung fun,* 火腿通粉, are favourites.

French toast: the Hong Kong version is a peanut butter sandwich, soaked in beaten egg, fried in oil, and served with heavy syrup and butter!

Toast topped with peanut butter and condensed milk is a particular favourite.

See mut nye cha, 絲襪奶茶, pantyhose milk tea. So-called because the tea is made using a long white cloth bag as a teabag, which looks a bit like a leg of pantyhose. Milk tea is a favourite of Hong Kong Cantonese. This one is a mix of black teas placed in the bag and boiled in a kettle for a minimum of eight minutes. The bag of tea leaves is pulled up and down several times to enhance flavour. The milk must be evaporated milk, not fresh milk or cream. Some people prefer condensed milk, and that style is called *cha jow*, 茶走, tea with something left out. The thing that is left out is the evaporated milk, which is replaced with condensed milk although this is not mentioned in the description of the drink. You just have to know the local custom.

Some restaurants are famous for their cold milk tea. This is a concoction of blocks of frozen milk tea and freshly made milk tea. The idea is to preserve the strength and thickness of the drink by using the milk tea ice blocks and not to dilute it with ordinary water ice.

Yewn yerng, 鴛鴦, literally Mandarin duck, is a mix of milk tea and coffee, served in the same cup. Mandarin ducks are renowned for their monogamous relationships and the drink is an auspicious symbol of togetherness. The term is also used to describe two kinds of similar ingredients served in a dish, in this case, the tea and coffee. For example, *yewn yerng fan*, 鴛鴦飯, is fried rice topped with both shredded chicken in tomato sauce, and with prawns in a cream sauce.

Many Cantonese believe that hot Coca-Cola cures the common cold. An infusion of fresh ginger boiled in Coke is a remedy for colds and a delicious drink.

Egg tart topped with bird's nest, *yeen wor darn tart*, 燕窩蛋撻.

Bor lor bow, 菠蘿包, a sweet bun with flaky topping. The uneven surface looks like pineapple, *bor lor*.

Gye may bow, 雞尾包, a sweet bun with coconut and custard butter cream. *Gye may* is a translation of cocktail, indicating the stuffing is a mixture.

Although these last three are very sweet pastries, Cantonese like to comment "it's nice, not very sweet," almost as an excuse for ordering the sugary excess.

Cantonese are also particularly fond of a pastry which is not sweet: *jew jye bow*, 豬仔包, literally piggy bun. It boasts a puffed-up crisp crust, and is based on the plain yeast bun, brioche, found in Portugal, Spain, and France. It is often stuffed with a piece of pork chop, *jew pa bow*, 豬扒包, and is an invention of the Macau Chinese.

Table manners

Chinese think nothing of spitting out food they do not want to swallow. There is usually a plate to hold the leftovers in more proper Chinese restaurants. Otherwise the food is spat directly onto the tablecloth. Waiters circulate to change plates, bowls, and spoons from time to time, especially after soupy or heavily sauced dishes and dishes with bones or shells.

Eating with your mouth open or talking with your mouth full is considered rude in traditional Chinese culture.

Few Chinese are taught how to use a knife and fork with the result that either one is used to convey food to the mouth. They tend to be held like chopsticks, which looks decidedly odd, and are often waved about like pointers through the meal. It is considered very rude to use chopsticks this way, but the prohibition does not seem to extend to knives, forks and spoons. Again, it is a matter of lack of education.

Western approaches to table manners vary from continent to continent. What might be accepted practice in America is viewed with horror in Australia and taken as offensive in Europe. By the same token, some of the strictures of fine European dining are unknown in other parts of the world. Who takes the first mouthful? Should I cut bread on my side plate? Should I move my plate away when I've finished eating? From which side should I expect my meal to be served? It is a minefield for the unwary.

The next time you are offended by the behaviour of diners at the next table it might help to remember that the problem is one of education and tradition. Then again, you might find that you want to get up and leave the restaurant, or change your seat, rather than look at a superbly turned out young woman eating off her knife.

Left handedness

Left handedness is seen as being contrary to the general line, creating difficulties in future life. All Chinese tools are designed to be used right-handedly. Even chopsticks are believed to be designed for right-handed use.

As a result, children who use their left hands have traditionally been nagged until they stop. Young parents are becoming increasingly tolerant of left-handedness.

Sharing dishes

Chinese food is designed to be shared. In Western restaurants, dishes may be put in the middle of the table, with diners helping themselves, or shovelling parts of meals onto others' plates. The fact that the chef has carefully planned each meal with a view to nutritional balance and pleasing presentation for one diner is not taken into account. This is an example of cross-culturalism which does not seem to work.

Service levels

In local Chinese restaurants, the major expectations are speed and accuracy. Sadly, they are seldom found.

Speed will generally be provided by the waiter being direct to the point of rudeness. "You sit here," with a finger pointing at a particular chair, is a common ploy. The waiter will then stand beside the table waiting for your order. If you ask to, *shock, horror!,* look at the menu, do not be surprised if staff just walk away, giving every evidence of annoyance.

Once you have decided and signal the waiter for attention, he or she may be reluctant to return, and may make you wait while ostentatiously looking for the order book.

Food, once ordered, is expected to arrive at the table, piping hot, within five minutes. Diners check the time and expect their order to be the next one dealt with by the kitchen. Being kept waiting is very annoying and, if a later arriving table seems to be getting preferential service, the reaction is likely to be both vocal and angry.

The moment one's eating tools are put down, the waiter collects your dishes without asking. If one practises standard European manners, where it is considered rude either to hold your eating tools all the time, or to clear one person's place while the others are still eating, then one is going to be offended.

This habit frequently annoys Cantonese diners as well, who may be saving the best mouthful for last. It is a sad fact that the high standard of table service which used to be typical in Hong Kong is now rare. Like so many other things in today's society, it is a matter of lack of training. Hong Kong lost many of its good waiters to Mainland China where their skills as staff trainers are in great demand. They are paid more than they can earn in Hong Kong where the profession does not command much respect.

Regular customers can expect better service and preferential treatment, even larger servings and better food.

Useful gestures

Tapping the table with the first two fingers of the right hand, bent, so that the action imitates kneeling and bowing to the Emperor. This indicates thanks for serving tea (only) and is a proper gesture of thanks for this service from a fellow diner, not a waiter.

The story behind the gesture is that the Emperor Qian Long, of the Qing dynasty, wanted to go out among the people *incognito*. The courtiers accompanying him were forbidden to kowtow or in any way mark him out as leader. They invented this way of showing their appreciation when their high and mighty Lord so abased himself as to serve them, who should properly have been serving him.

Circling your index finger downwards towards the table while holding your hand in the air means please bring my bill.

In the old days, bills *per se* were not presented but the empty dishes were left on the table. Each different dish, whether of size or decoration, was in a single price category. The total owing was then shouted across the room to the cashier and the diner would walk over to pay his bill before leaving the restaurant.

Charged extras

Wet towels, peanuts or pickles, chilli sauce or mustard, and tea, are all extras which you should expect to have added to your bill. Tea is charged by the number of people at the table, not by the amount consumed. The only exception is in cheap restaurants where all of these frills either are offered *gratis* to the customer or are not available.

Tipping

A 10% service charge is the rule, rather than the exception, on restaurant bills. On top of that, Cantonese generally tip the service staff a small amount up to the closest round number, generally between HK$20 and HK$30.

If the bill is quite large, say for a banquet or a group of ten or fifteen, the tip will be proportionally larger, reflecting the extra level of service received. On a bill of HK$4,000, for instance, the tip might be HK$200.

Regular customers show their thanks at Chinese New Year by taking red packets to their favourite waiters or waitresses.

If paying by credit card it is normal to give the tip in cash. This is to ensure that the staff receive it, and that it does not go into the restaurant's general revenue.

Paying the bill

Cantonese think nothing of making a scene as they fight over who is going to pay for the meal. People sneak over to the reception or cash desk on a pretext in order to get in first. When later it is suggested that the bill be called for, the "winner" can smirk and say, no, I've paid it!

When the waiter brings the folder to the table with the bill, it is customary for the male diners to all try to put down a credit card or to fling cash at the waiter.

Women dining amongst themselves are most likely to split the bill. In mixed-sex dinners, a woman might take charge and say, "let's split the bill," and immediately collect a proportionate amount from each diner or couple. This is considered quite acceptable, whereas if a man made the same suggestion, he would lose face and be seen as a cheapskate.

27

PUBLIC TRANSPORT AND TAXIS

Taxis

Taxi licences – there are four types of taxi licence granted in Hong Kong.

Red taxis are licensed to travel anywhere in the territory but are regionally based and the drivers may only have road knowledge of that region. There is no physical distinction between the cars and a Hong Kong Island-based taxi driver may not accept fares outside his area; the same goes for Kowloon peninsula drivers. Legally, taxi drivers might be bound to accept the fare and take you where you want to go. If they do not want to cross the harbour, however, you will be unceremoniously asked to leave the vehicle.

Cross-harbour trips charge double the tunnel fee for crossing the harbour. This takes into account the possibility of an empty return trip. Taxis wishing to return to their regional base offer a "discounted" price of a single tunnel fare. There are special ranks for taxis looking for passengers who wish to cross the harbour and taxis at those ranks will not take you on a local trip.

Green taxis are restricted to travel within the New Territories and you must change vehicles if you wish to travel outside the region.

Blue taxis are restricted to travel on Lantau Island. They may not cross the Tsing Yi Bridge.

Hailing a taxi – stick your arm straight out and flap your hand from the wrist. This is the recognised gesture to hail a taxi in Hong Kong.

Taxis are not supposed to stop on double yellow lines but this restriction was waived during the SARS epidemic and has not been rigorously enforced since. There is no way of telling whether a driver will stop or not, it seems to depend on his or her mood.

If you see a red "out of service" card placed over the "for hire" flag, it is either an indication that the driver is not accepting fares because his shift has ended, for instance, or that vehicle is on the "wrong" side of the harbour. 3-4pm is shift changeover time and it can be difficult to secure a taxi at this time.

If you want to cross the harbour, hail a taxi using a dipping motion of the hand, simulating the trip under the harbour. This indicates to the driver that it is worth his while to stop and pick you up.

Stopping a taxi – it is a problem with language that causes taxi drivers to slam on the brakes when asked to "stop here, please." Chinese passengers always give the driver warning that they wish to alight.

Westerners find themselves in a Catch 22. Without fluency in Cantonese, they are seldom able to give this sort of advance warning. Even if they are fluent, the driver may not "hear" that Cantonese is being spoken or not understand the instruction. Thus, when asked to "stop here" drivers become angry at the apparent thoughtlessness of the passenger who has not considered road safety and suddenly wants to get out. So he slams on the brakes.

Giving the destination – English place names for different areas, buildings, streets, districts, etc., of Hong Kong are often vastly different from the Cantonese place names.

The same rules of language apply as in earlier chapters and the "sounds-like" transliterations of the names of some places from Cantonese into English cause problems of their own.

In Cantonese, there is no initial "sh" sound. A taxi driver asked to take a passenger to Sheung Wan, Sham Shui Po, or Shau Kei Wan has to first translate the address in his head. If he cannot understand the passenger, he may use his radio to call base for assistance and ask the passenger to repeat his destination into the microphone.

"D" and "t" confusions also abound. As to g-k, b-p, and the intricacies of "ts" and "ch", these are sounds which most Westerners just cannot make. Some are aspirated, some are not. To the Cantonese ear, it sounds so completely different that the place names are not recognised. Tsim Sha Tsui, 尖沙咀, in Cantonese sounds more like *Jeem Sa Joy*.

The ends of lines on the MTR are good examples of the difficulties of transliteration. Chai Wan, Wan Chai, Sheung Wan, and Tsuen Wan sound in Cantonese like *Chye Wan,* 柴灣, *Wan Jye,* 灣仔, *Serng Wan,* 上環, and *Chewn Wan,* 荃灣, respectively.

Some English place names bear no relevance to the Cantonese names for the same places. Stanley in Cantonese is *Chek Chew,* 赤柱, "red pole", which refers to a long-gone kapok tree; Causeway Bay is *Tuung Lor Wan,* 銅鑼灣, "bronze gong bay," referring to the original shape of the bay; Admiralty is *Gum Juung,* 金鐘, "gold bell," referring to a naval base no longer situated there; and Aberdeen is *Herng Gong Jye,* 香港仔, "little Hong Kong," in memory of the first landing place of the British.

The same rule applies to some buildings and location destinations. Pacific Place in Cantonese is *Tye Gwoo Gwong Cherng,* 太古廣場, "Swire Square," as Swire Properties is the developer; Festival Walk is *Yow Yut Sing,* 又一城, "Another One City," after the district Yau Yat Chuen, *Yow Yut Chewn,* 又一村.

Mong Kok – in Cantonese the place name is *Wong Gok,* 旺角. Of two differing explanations for the difference, the first is that the area used to be called *Mong Gok,* 網角, Fishing Net Point, when it was a seaside village. When the Chinese name was changed to *Wong Gok,* Prosperous Point (after land reclamation it was no longer a seaside location) the English name was not changed.

The other explanation deals with British government officers who travelled around Hong Kong asking about place names from the locals for mapping purposes. The handwritten notes were given to local staff members to produce street signs. A semi-literate workman put the "W" upside down so that *Wong Kok* became *Mong Kok*.

Public transport

Eating and drinking are prohibited on all forms of public transport. Cantonese treat eating and drinking very differently from Westerners and tend to ignore these restrictions. If hungry, they eat. If thirsty, they drink. Other passengers seldom complain unless there are strong aromas.

On all public transport, aisle seats are preferred so that the rider will not have to manoeuvre across a stranger when alighting. Also, window seats may be hotter and expose the passenger to direct sunshine, not a desirable condition.

When you board a bus, the only seats left may be by the window and gaining access can be difficult. Do not expect Cantonese to move over and make way for you. They will not. Nor will they stand to let you get past. They will, however, move their legs to one side, or pull them up to their chests, to facilitate passage.

Bus and train drivers do not wait for all passengers to be safely seated before moving off. This is one reason often given for not standing to allow ease of access to the inner seats.

Most public transport now accepts **Octopus cards**. These pre-paid cards can be purchased at MTR stations from the customer service booths; they can be topped up at various outlets such as supermarkets and convenience stores. You can also use the card to purchase goods and services in various outlets.

Some banks and service providers also issue Octopus cards which are personalised and are automatically recharged by bank transfer as the stored value is used. Each recharge is $250 and up to three recharges per day are currently allowed. If you lose your card, it will not be immediately cancelled when you report the loss. For administrative reasons the supplier insists on an end-of-day rule. Thus if a dishonest person picks up your card they can spend up to HK$1,000 before the company will no longer hold you liable for the purchases.

Buses

There are hints to the destinations or routes revealed in the bus numbers. Route numbers ending in M or K – 12M, 81K, etc. – go past MTR stations. The K is an obsolete reference to a train system.

Most buses cease service at midnight. For a greater fare, some buses run at night and these are designated N before the route number: N171, N8, etc.

Express routes may have the designation X (eXpress), P (exPress), or R (Rapid): 30X, 8P, 88R, etc. Express does not mean non-stop. It refers to the route taken which may be partly via freeway where there are no bus stops. Once off the freeway the bus operates as normal. Express buses which do not have a letter designation have a route number with three numerals where the first numeral is not 1, 6, or 9 – 592, 788, etc.

Cross-harbour tunnel buses also have three numerals in their route number. The routes which go through the central tunnel start with 1, buses which use the Western tunnel start with 9 and those using the Eastern tunnel start with 6 – 112, 973, 680, etc.

Route numbers designated A, B, C, or D with the same number indicate variations in route with only some sections in common. For instance, 23 goes all the way from North Point to Pokfield Road in Pok Fu Lam. 23A goes only from Tai Hang to Robinson Road in Mid-Levels and then continues back to Tai Hang in a loop. 23B goes between Braemar Hill and Park Road, Mid-Levels, in a loop.

Mini buses

These vehicles are often owner-operated or belong to a private micro-bus company. They must be licensed to operate as public transport carriers. While they follow fixed routes, there are no formal bus stops and no formal methods of letting the driver know that you wish to alight.

To hail a mini bus, wave at it, as if it were a taxi. The driver puts a sign in the window when the bus is full. If you are in a group of four and there are only three spaces left, the driver will only allow three of you to board. This rule is strictly applied. Standing is not permitted. Young children ride free if they sit on a lap.

To get the bus to stop, passengers shout at the driver that they wish to alight at a particular spot down the road. Shouting at the last minute is not welcomed and the problem of language raises its head again. If you are not fluent in Cantonese, it can be difficult. Try "please will you let me off at the next corner, *gye how yow lok,* 街口有落". The driver waves his left hand to indicate that he has heard the request.

There are two types of mini bus: red and green.

Red mini buses are privately owned, often by the driver, which explains the personalisation of the driver's cabin with stereos, statuettes, etc.

They may change the termini within their routes depending on traffic conditions, demand, roadworks, etc.

There is no fixed timetable and no fixed price. The driver determines this. For instance, if a typhoon signal 8 is up, the fare might triple; during peak hours the fare might be higher; in slow periods the driver might lower the fare and will also drive more slowly, trawling for custom. The drivers give change and the fare can be paid on leaving the vehicle. This is changing and it is more common now to pay as you enter using your Octopus card.

Once his bus is full, the driver generally drives as fast as he can. It can be quite hairy. A wry Cantonese saying is that the rate for a red mini bus is the fare plus your life!

Green mini buses are company-owned. The routes are put out to tender on a regular basis and the drivers are company employees. The routes are numbered.

Fares are set by the company and are paid as you enter. No change is offered and if you do not have the right change it is quite acceptable to hold out your 20-dollar note, say, and boarding passengers will then understand that you are asking them to help you with change. The normal reaction is that they give their fare to you. When you have collected enough fares to

equal 20 dollars (don't forget to include your own fare), put it in the fare collection slot.

The drivers are paid a wage and are less inclined to speed when the bus is full or to trawl for custom when business is slow. There are timetables for the routes but these are not a matter of public information. Rather they are used for reasons of internal control.

MTR, Mass Transit Railway

Carriages are extraordinarily well kept and passengers treat them as if they were part of their home. It is most unusual to see rubbish left behind by passengers and the HK$1,500 littering fine in Hong Kong applies on the MTR as well as on the street.

Each station displays information about the line it serves, the opening and closing times of the station, and the expected time of departure of the next train. On festival days the trains may run all night or with greater frequency at peak times.

Generally, any passenger seen to have a greater need will be offered a seat: those with young children, pregnant women, the elderly, and the disabled.

On escalators within the concourses, and now in other parts of Hong Kong as well, you are invited to stand on the right and walk on the left. Tourists standing on the left of escalators, and therefore blocking the walkway, will get short shrift from other users.

The entrances to MTR stations are also often marked for foot traffic. Signs indicating that you should keep to the left or right are painted on the footway, stairs, and adjacent walls. There does not seem to be a fixed rule for this. In Central MTR station, for instance, you are invited to walk on the left at some entrances and on the right at other entrances.

Mid-Levels Escalator

A free public escalator connects the new Star Ferry pier on the Hong Kong waterfront with Conduit Road in the Mid-Levels.

This is a series of short escalators and travelators going up the side of the hill, connected by walkways, some of which are sky bridges over busy roads. The escalators run downhill in the morning from 6 am until 10 am and uphill from 10 am until they shut down at about 1 am. A set of stairs runs beside it for foot traffic going in the other direction, or for use when the escalators are shut for maintenance.

Maintenance takes place during open hours so it is usual to find one section of the escalator closed as the maintenance team works its way from the bottom to the top and then starts again at the beginning.

Signs on the side of the passenger way invite users to stand on the right and walk on the left. There is a constant stream of people using the transport and you may be shouted at or shoved out of the way by regular users if you ignore these strictures.

Ferries

Ferries to outlying islands are owned by various companies and the Star Ferry Company only covers cross-harbour routes.

All outlying island routes have a higher weekend fare, as much as twice the weekday rate. Monthly tickets are available for residents.

Sampans

Sampans are available for private travel and inter-island crossings from private operators. The sampans are government licensed to carry passengers but there are no set fares. Each journey's fare must be negotiated between the operator and the intending passenger. Bargaining is expected. Negotiate before you set out on the journey, as you have no bargaining power once the journey is complete!

28

PERCEPTION OF TIME

Hong Kong people are proud of their efficiency. Proud of the amount they can get done in one day, it is said that to replace one Hong Kong Chinese you need to pay three other people.

Chinese consider queuing up to be a waste of time. On the Star Ferry, for instance, people crowd the gangway long before the ferry reaches the pier. Ferry staff have their work cut out to restrain the eager crowd and ensure safety.

When returning from Macau, a disorderly stampede to immigration involves pushing and shoving and utter disregard of the comfort of others as each Chinese strives to get there first. As Hong Kong's immigration is already the fastest in the world, taking less than two minutes for local residents, this makes little sense. It is best to steer clear; the lame, the cripple, the halt, you will all be run down as the natural mannerliness and care of strangers deserts them in this lemming-like rush.

Chinese feel there is some shame involved in being the last in a queue. All the worst aspects of character come to the fore as friends or family members invite latecomers to jump the queue, which in turn creates ill-feeling in those behind. Often the latecomers are the young children, the elderly, the pregnant, all those who could not keep up with the unseemly rush; this stops the situation from getting out of hand as tempers are damped by a natural respect for those in need.

A nursery rhyme deals best with the feelings engendered by "slowness" and "lastness".

Harng duck fye ho sye gye, 行得快好世界

Harng duck mor mo bay gor, 行得魔冇鼻哥

Walk fast good world, walk slow have no nose.

Here the idiom about the nose is the Chinese habit of pointing to the nose when referring to oneself. Therefore, no nose means low self-esteem and being seen as inferior.

Telling the time

Unlike the Chinese precision when talking about price, telling the time is a very relaxed business.

Minutes are treated in units of five. The numbers of the clock face are used for reference and one (o'clock) is used to mean five minutes, two to mean ten minutes, etc. So 3:15 becomes *sarm deem sarm,* 三點三, three o'clock three. This is a good time for afternoon tea (taken earlier in Hong Kong than in England) but do not be surprised if your Cantonese guests are late. Fifteen minutes is only three – it is no big deal!

More often, the minutes are just omitted when stating the time. 4:14, 4:35, or 4:45 are all expressed the same way, as after four o'clock, *say deem gay*, 四點幾, four o'clock more.

The same formula is used for the duration of time. Five minutes is *yut gor jee* 一個字, one character (dot or spot on the clock face); 10 minutes is *lerng gor jee* 兩個字, two characters; 15 minutes is *sarm gor jee* 三個字, three characters. 30 minutes is the exception that proves the rule, it is half an hour, *boon gor juung* 半個鐘 (not *look gor jee,* 六個字, six characters).

How far is too far?

Cantonese are used to being next door to the places they visit. They tend to consider that if for any reason a trip will take over 40 minutes, it is just too far.

The outlying districts are worlds of their own with residents seldom travelling out of their comfort zone and strangers seldom coming in.

Day trips are another matter altogether. To hop on a bus or train to go up to Shenzhen is a popular outing – while to say you are going to Lamma Island, a shorter journey, for the day would draw comments of surprise and questions as to why you would spend so much time travelling!

Telling distance, asking directions

Chinese are more likely to tell you how long it will take to walk or drive to a destination – not how many blocks, miles, or kilometres you must travel.

If you ask for directions, a Cantonese will typically point you in the general direction and tell you what shop you will see as you approach. You are then expected to ask someone else. It is believed that people cannot remember directions for more than a few minutes. If pressed for more precise directions, it is very rare that a Cantonese could tell you how many sets of traffic lights you must pass, exactly where you should turn, or what the distance is in terms of length.

Blaring car horns

Hong Kong drivers lean on the horn at the first sign of a traffic jam. The traffic in Hong Kong actually flows very freely. It is fast and well ordered in the main, and perhaps because of this, the impatience of drivers is on a knife edge.

Horns are also used by one driver to express his dislike of another driver's poor practice. It is one of the less pleasant aspects of Hong Kong life but does not extend to physical violence or road rage.

Repairs, service technicians and delivery services

Cantonese expect to be able to ring and have a technician complete the repairs necessary on their home appliances, etc., on the same day.

It doesn't happen.

Generally, service companies make an appointment and nominate morning or afternoon for the visit, but not more accurately than that. Depending on their workload, the technicians may be running hours late. They do not, however, think to call and let you know. The result is that the householder has to ring the company again, often having to endure the automatic queuing system – now press 1, now press 6, now press 5, now press 6 – Aaaaaugh!! The response when it comes is usually unhelpful and the operator will not give out the technicians' mobile phone numbers.

Technicians are in the habit of ringing the next householder on his list, giving only 15 or 20 minutes' warning of his or her impending arrival, so you have little choice but to sit at home and wait.

Delivery services work on much the same lines. Whether it is a new sofa from a furniture shop or groceries from the supermarket, you will be given a guestimate of the arrival time and must wait. Most buildings have security doors and while some building watchmen will take delivery for you, this is not the norm and is often prohibited.

Interior decorators

There are some fabulous contractors in Hong Kong; there are also many crooks. So be careful when looking at quotes and always include a time clause in the contract if you want the work finished on time.

Contractors often work on a very slim margin and are reluctant to knock back work, with the result that they may be overstretched or not have the right tools or sufficient workmen to do the job. This is exacerbated by seasonal concerns as very few people want work done during the month of Chinese New Year, and in the humid periods paint does not dry, etc., so work tends to tail off.

The first week sees the contractor rush in with great energy, bring in more materials than you could believe possible, and make quick inroads into the job. During the next week, first one, then another, worker will disappear as he goes off to work on another site, leaving only one or two at your site, who often cannot cope with the necessary work. As the penalties of the time clause loom, an influx of workers descends and they may work 24 hours a day to get the contract completed. This last-minute rush often results in shoddy workmanship and lack of attention to detail – no handles on the cupboards, no hangers for artwork, etc.

Local wisdom is not to pay the full contract price up front. Generally, it is not expected and, if you do pay first, you run the risk of being so far down the list of priorities that your job may not be attended to this year or next!

A city that never sleeps

Hong Kong people see themselves as an active people who are always looking for something to do and keep their schedule full from morning to night. Well, that is the Chinese point of view. After some time living in Hong Kong, foreigners can be heard to say, "He won't do it unless he's specifically told to," or, "What? Why pick something up and carry it when you can drag it!" These expressions refer to what people from a different culture see as a poor work ethic or laziness. It is more a difference in attitude, a cultural divide, which does not lend itself to easy comparison.

Old age does not see graceful retirement from the scene. If less sleep is now needed, the elderly congregate in public parks for exercise, in tea houses for conversation, and take advantage of day tours and discounts for pensioners at museums and other places of interest and entertainment. At 5am in any public park groups of elderly people, often in their pyjamas, can be found engaged in Chinese chess, exercise, walking their caged birds, or other social pursuits.

Children are kept busy from the moment they are born. Parents run themselves ragged taking them from one extra-curricular class to another. Pregnant women might also attend some of these classes so that the unborn child gets used to the idea that life is going to be an endless opportunity to learn.

Teenagers and young people centre their life on food. Alcohol is not a big item on the agenda, nor is dancing. Karaoke bars and late-night snack outlets, open until 2 or 3am, abound. Teenagers may not take much exercise but they do like to stay up late and sleep in if they can.

Restaurants are open all day long. Many operate on a 24-hour schedule. Once the lunch crowd has left at 2pm, for instance, the prices are lowered to attract customers for afternoon tea. In Hong Kong, afternoon tea consists of *dim sum*, noodles and dumplings, pies and pastries, and chicken wings and legs, etc., rather than the Western spread of cakes and sandwiches.

29

ON THE STREET

Mye kay chow foon, 賣旗籌款, sticker selling

Over recent years, the budget in Hong Kong has been slashed for charitable organisations. Handouts from the Government, the Hong Kong Jockey Club, charitable arms of large companies and religious bodies, or quangos such as the Community Chest, cannot fill all of the requirements.

One method of fundraising common to many charitable bodies is to apply to the Government for a licence to sell "flags" on the street. "Flag" refers to the original feathers on a pin now replaced by an adhesive sticker emblazoned with the logo of the charity. The licences are generally granted for the morning only and the "flags" are sold by volunteers, often schoolchildren in uniform. The elderly are also pressed into service as their very appearance plays upon the heartstrings of the passers-by.

Stickers are now sold outside MTR entrances (the volunteers are forbidden to use MTR property) as well as the more traditional Star Ferry environs and at any place where people congregate and may have a few moments to spare – for example larger pedestrian crossings and bus stops.

The price of stickers is not fixed, a donation is requested. Receipts are not given. Commonly, spare coins, two and five dollar coins being the most usual, are given. The volunteer offering the flags is not permitted to handle the money in any way, so no change can be given, and the donor must put the money directly into the collection purse which is designed to easily accept either coins or notes. Once the money is placed in the bag the design is such that the cash can only be removed by destroying the bag.

Begging and busking

In Hong Kong, there is no tradition of street performance or street musicians. Anyone who plays a musical instrument in the street is seen as a beggar.

Beggars in Hong Kong work the public areas not routinely patrolled by the police and not in the direct control of building management officers. Aerial walkways between buildings, pedestrian subways, and footpaths near taxi ranks are the more common places.

Begging is a profession in Asia and many beggars are "owned" by organisations who arrange visas for the beggars, their accommodation, and the sites from which they operate. The beggars are "collected" and moved on to the next spot every few hours.

Some beggars have their regular spots and can be seen year after year. Westerners may "adopt" a particular beggar whom they pass on a daily basis but the Chinese think this should not be encouraged and that the beggars are already making a good living and not paying tax or office rent. When setting up their pitch, beggars generally place a few coins or notes of the denomination they expect so that the passers by have an indication of what to give.

Hand gestures

Hand signals are used to represent numbers, especially in street markets where it might be difficult to hear the exact rate being quoted. (See following page). This is quite common in Asian countries but the gestures in each region vary slightly.

When being photographed, Cantonese are prone to making fun of each other by holding a thumb up above another's head as a representation of a deer or goat horn. This is not meant to be insulting and should not be taken as such, it is just in fun.

Another common gesture is the V sign. This signifies victory and happiness. It does not mean "up yours" (whichever way the palm is facing)!

Upstairs shopping and services

Street-level rentals in Hong Kong are very expensive so many retail outlets operate from office and apartment buildings, not all of them properly licensed!

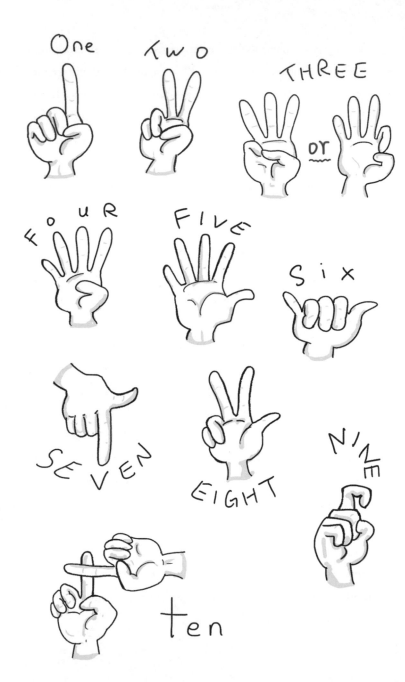

Beauticians, spas, foot massage practitioners, restaurants, hairdressers, clothing shops, bookshops, specialist food suppliers, optometrists, and many other businesses are run from upstairs.

Many are run as clubs without charge for membership. This is of significance in restaurants as food and liquor can then be sold under a club licence. Restrictions apply, but these should not affect the user, just the operator. Most of these restaurants advertise themselves as "private kitchens" and some of them are very good indeed. They cover a wide range of cuisines.

Discounts – a seasonal game

There are seasonal discounts in all retail shops, especially in December/January/February and in July. As the sale time draws to a close, the discounts increase but the range of goods on offer lessens.

Sales are organised quite strictly into categories: pre-sale for card holders and members, first reduction of 10-20% for the general public, second reduction of 30%, and final reduction of 50%.

Many retail outlets have a discount corner, or shelf, where everyday bargains are to be had. Banks and credit card companies often team up with particular retailers or restaurants to give discounts to their cardholders. It is quite acceptable to ask your friends if they have discount or VIP cards at this or that retailer and ask to access their discount.

Even though it is against the rules of most private clubs, it is not considered in any way offensive to ask your friend to take you to his club and then reimburse him for the bill. Similarly, it is quite acceptable to ask the waiter which card has a discount deal today so that you can get the best possible deal for the service. There is no shame whatsoever attached to such a request.

Shop assistants

It is considered very polite and good salesmanship to not leave a customer alone to browse. This can annoy people who are not accustomed to the habit and lead to feelings that you are being watched in case you are light-fingered. No such offence is intended. It is just a different culture at work.

The squat-upon vs. the sit-upon

Elderly Hong Kong locals and Mainland Chinese are accustomed to squat on the lavatory. Most public lavatories are of the "squatter" design which is considered more hygienic.

When these people use a Western lavatory, designed for sitting upon, they are very careful not to touch the seat with their bare flesh. Cantonese believe many serious diseases are passed on by indiscriminate use of public lavatories. Therefore, they either hover over, or squat on, the seat or the edge of the bowl, often leaving footprints to amuse the next user. It simply would not cross their minds to clean off these footprints; just as it would not cross their minds that they are not using the appliance in the manner in which it was designed to be used. Nor, sadly, does it occur to them to clean up after themselves if this misuse of the appliance results in spillage. That, also, is left for the next user to deal with – so beware!

There are many documented cases in which the unexpected strain put on the porcelain by squatting on a sit-upon has resulted in the bowl shearing off the wall and the user ending up in hospital with serious injuries.

Sleeping in public

On the park bench, on the train, in a bus – it is common to see Cantonese having a nap with no care that this might be something better done in private. In the morning the whole bus might be asleep on the way to work, though it is most unusual for the nappers to miss their stops. Woe betide you if you take a call on your mobile phone, expect the censure of the whole bus.

Especially after lunch, a short nap is considered healthy and it doesn't matter where you are, just get a few zzzs.

In many restaurants, particularly Western restaurants which are seldom open in the afternoon, waiters customarily make a bed of the banquettes or push a few chairs together to take an afternoon nap. Table cloths are used as blankets and to exclude the light. It looks like a clutch of caterpillar larvae.

In the office, it is quite common to see someone asleep on his or her desk. In some offices, people turn off the lights in the conference room and retire thence for a short nap.

Walk on the right, drive on the left

Hong Kong follows the British system and vehicles travel on the left of carriageways. If you are driving to China, and can get the necessary permits – not a simple matter – you will have to change at the border. In Mainland China vehicles travel on the right-hand side of the road.

In busy pedestrian areas, like Central and Causeway Bay, the local habit is to walk on the right side of footpaths. This is especially noticeable when it is raining.

Walking arm-in-arm down the street

Women in Hong Kong display friendship by linking arms as they walk down the footpath. This can be extremely vexing to other pedestrians, both Chinese and Western, because of the crowding in Hong Kong. Often they amble slowly, chatting and ignoring the rest of the world.

This is extremely out-of-character behaviour for Asians, who tend to be very aware of the people around them and care for the personal space and comfort of strangers as a matter of course.

The Cantonese reaction to this is to demand of the group: *Teeu gye nay mye jor ga?*, 條街你買咗喋?, When did you buy this street?

In Mainland China, men also link arms. This is not a matter of sexual preference, it is just a way that men display friendship in that society. It is not, however, so annoying as Mainland streets tend to be wider.

Umbrella and stroller etiquette

The use of umbrellas, backpacks, and strollers can cause difficulties for other pedestrians.

Men and women seem to ignore the fact that raising an **umbrella** to protect themselves from either the rain or the sun makes a difference to the space they take up – or that the spokes of the umbrella are at eye level of taller passers-by.

While you see Westerners taking note of other pedestrians as a matter of course, and moving their umbrella out of the way of others, Cantonese seldom pay attention to the lethal weapon they brandish to protect themselves from the elements.

On busy streets, in shops and supermarkets, and on public transport **backpacks** prove to be particularly troublesome. The wearers often seem to be unaware of the extra space their hump occupies or that they are crashing into the next person, often hurting them, or swiping things off shelves. Beware! Give backpack users a bit of space because they are not going to give it to you.

The problem with **strollers** may not be peculiar to Hong Kong. Modern Mums and Dads seem to have the idea that the world revolves around their offspring and expect everyone else to make way for them.

Traditional Chinese child-minding techniques do not include strollers, but rely on baby harnesses, *mair dye*, 孭帶 and many footpaths in Hong Kong are not sufficiently wide or level for the smooth progress of strollers, pushers, and baby carriages. This results in child carers having to either push all the other pedestrians out of the way in order to get from A to B, or take the child carrier onto the vehicle roadway.

The same problems apply to wheelchair users who often find that they must join the traffic on the road as footpaths cease to be navigable for all sorts of reasons. A tree may have grown to block access, there may be roadworks which do not take into account the use of wheelchairs or push chairs, or there may be deliveries piled outside a business waiting to be moved.

The use of strollers is also creating a problem in restaurants as increasing numbers of diners expect their strollers to be accommodated while they are dining. Many parents then expect to be able to let down the stroller into a bed so that their precious bundle can kick his or her legs, play with toys, or get some sleep. There simply is not the room and this leads to bad feelings and often expressions of anger, both from the other diners and from restaurant staff. The comfort of the other diners is not ignored, it is more a matter of expediency, and of there being nowhere else to safely leave the child.

Brrr...

Air conditioning in public areas is incredibly cold. The Government standard is 25.5°C but most thermostats are set at 18-20°C and often lower. It is thought that the lower temperature will attract customers to shopping malls and that this edge will be lost by following the guidelines. Cantonese tend to set the thermostat in hotel rooms to 15°C. A study on buses recorded 15°C in summer and 12°C in winter.

For this reason, you see people with jackets if they have to travel for more than 10 minutes. In offices and schools, sweaters are worn all year round.

In Hong Kong a cold weather warning is issued at 15°C, and locals bring out their padded jackets and fur coats. Hot weather warnings are issued at 33°C.

30

PROSTITUTION

It is neither against the law in Hong Kong to prostitute oneself nor to avail oneself of the services of a prostitute.

Soliciting is against the laws of Hong Kong and so is living off the earnings of a prostitute. It is also illegal, both in Hong Kong and in China, to directly enquire how much a person charges (for prostitution services).

In Hong Kong a prostitute is known as a chicken, *gye*, 雞, because in Mandarin the word for chicken sounds like the word for prostitute (chicken, *ji*, 雞 and prostitute, *ji*, 妓) and Cantonese avoid, wherever possible, offering offence by direct description of something that may be considered shameful or offensive.

To visit a prostitute is to call a chicken or to order chicken, *geeu gye*, 叫雞.

Yut low yut fuung, 一樓一鳳, one apartment one phoenix, is the most common form of prostitution. One simply rents a flat and goes into business. The prostitute is called *fuung jair*, 鳳姐, young female phoenix, and advertises in adult magazines giving the address. Red paper and/or red lights are displayed at the door to the apartment.

This can be confusing as red lights are also used in domestic shrines for ancestor worship.

Advertising includes euphemistic words like *Seeu Seeu Jair,* 蕭 小姐, Miss Siu. Siu is a common surname which also sounds like the word for flute (*seeu,* 簫) and indicates that oral sex is provided.

A name may include the word lotus, *leen,* 蓮, which sounds like *leen* (no character exists) and means breast. Big breast is always the eye-catching word on signs, and very often the name lotus goes along with description of big breast, *Dye bor seeu foo,* 大波 少婦, big breasted young woman.

Yellow and/or purple signs, often lit, which include addresses and names like these can be taken to be advertisements for prostitution.

Another popular way of hiring a prostitute is to go to a motel with rooms to rent by the hour. The reception desk can be asked to telephone a *ma larm,* 馬欖, horse stable. This is an escort service with pimps, *ma foo,* 馬伕, (horseman, rider) who will bring the prostitute to the room, collect the money, and ensure the safety of the prostitute.

Many prostitutes are under-age and/or visitors to Hong Kong on tourist visas. The horse stables have a constantly changing supply of young women for their clientele.

More mature or more presentable prostitutes go to bars, nightclubs and some karaoke bars to seduce customers themselves and then perform their services in hotels and motels. For cost effectiveness, many form into small groups of four or five and rent a semi-permanent room in the better hotels. When one has a customer, the others leave.

Other services, including oral sex and masturbation, are provided in saunas, massage parlours, internet cafés, and karaoke bars.

Da fay gay, 打飛機, shoot down the aeroplane, is a euphemism for masturbatory sex services. Massage parlours specialising in this are known as airports, *fay gay cherng*, 飛機場 (the same euphemism used for flat-chested women).

A man who hires more than one prostitute at a time is *yut wong yee how*, 一王二后, one king two queens; or *hay serng fay*, 起雙飛, lifting double wings, a play on words of the chicken allusion.

Short-term mistresses: many men import women on tourist visas from the mainland and keep them in Hong Kong for a few months. The men usually find the women in private membership clubs on the mainland and the women often know each other and socialise together in Hong Kong. They dress expensively and haunt the more expensive hotels for high tea, and the more expensive boutiques, while their patrons are busy earning the money to pay for their services.

Prostitution for non-Chinese is readily available in bars and nightclubs, particularly in Wan Chai. Some of these establishments display pictures outside the door of the class of girl you are encouraged to think you will find inside; some have the Mama San and a couple of good-looking women sitting on chairs outside the bar encouraging passers-by to enter.

Korean and Japanese men in Hong Kong can be quite xenophobic in their choice of prostitute and import women of their own nationality especially for the purpose. Again, the women come in on tourist visas and the police tend to leave them alone.

"Promotion companies" bring groups of girls into Hong Kong, mainly from the Philippines. These women undergo three to six months training in dancing and talking to customers at the bar; they are legally employed as entertainers. They are strictly controlled, live in dormitories, and are not free to walk around by themselves. They are well fed and cared for and may be allowed out in groups of three or more for recreation.

Inside some nightclubs, you may see full encounter sex in the form of "lap dancing." If you are just looking for a drink late at night there are plenty of bars where that sort of behaviour is not tolerated.

A recent addition to the ranks is "tourists" or women on two-week visas. The prettier ones seem to be allowed three or four tourist visas of two weeks each time and they work mainly for drink percentages. They do not operate under the protection of a Mama San and no bar fine is payable. Payment is by negotiation.

On Sundays and other days on which domestic helpers have a holiday it is difficult to find the "tourist" class of prostitute. Many off-duty maids like to make extra money on the side by prostitution, or are just looking for company and the illusion of affection and do not charge for sex, although this is becoming rare. Stories abound of these women taking their customers back to their employers' flats and conducting their business there, particularly when the employer is out of town.

When a US navy vessel is due in town for shore leave an influx of women from mainland China, Thailand, and the Philippines arrive in Hong Kong on tourist visas. They can easily earn a decent profit on top of their fares.

A particularly unpleasant class of pimp has sprung up since 2005, the so-called "managers." These women are retired prostitutes who bring in new operators whom they strictly, often violently, control, and for whose services they charge very high prices. Often these prostitutes come back to Hong Kong later as "tourists" on their own initiative and operate as freelancers.

Male prostitution

Male prostitutes are called *ngarp*, 鴨, duck.

They usually work out of a *ngarp deem*, 鴨店, duck bar, where the women choose the men who display themselves to the best advantage. Most *ngarp* are from mainland China or Thailand. The female customers come from all spectra of the community.

The women, after paying a bar fine, usually take the men to a hotel.

A small group of women may join together to hire the services of one man for either group or serial sex.

Ballroom dancing teachers can be a front for prostitution and after a few dance classes you may be offered more. In Shenzhen there are ballrooms with both male and female teachers for rent by the hour; generally the female teachers do not offer sexual services and this may well be because the male customers are actually interested in dance lessons.

Female customers often strike up longer-term relationships with their instructors. One, or in some cases a few women, might rent a flat for the teacher and pay his living expenses.

Some women import a dance partner to Hong Kong for a period of a week or a month. They accommodate them and expect them to be on hand for dancing at all hours. These are often middle-aged women who are truly interested in ballroom dancing but the teachers are generally in their twenties and the feeling is that more than dancing is involved.

Golf instruction in Shenzhen is often a euphemism for male prostitution.

Homosexual prostitution

The very little paid homosexual prostitution in Hong Kong is much the same as elsewhere in the world: rent boys advertise in gay magazines.

Various bars, nightclubs, and saunas cater to those of same-sex proclivities and these are used as pick-up joints for casual sex. Certain male public lavatories in Hong Kong are best avoided by those who may be offended by public homosexual contact.

31

OFFENSIVE BEHAVIOUR IN PUBLIC

Nose and ear picking

Public nose or ear picking is more a male pastime than a female one among the Chinese. There is no thought that this is something better kept to the confines of one's own bathroom (with the door shut). Chinese women often complain that the habit is disgusting but this has done little to curb it. Some men even grow their little finger nails long, the better to probe these orifices. Young Chinese women put these habits on the list of things unacceptable in a boyfriend.

Scratching, face picking

Cantonese, if confronted with a moment of inactivity, check their faces with their hands to see if all is in order, particularly the area beneath the chin. If something untoward is found, a spot, a stray hair, for example, a seemingly uncontrollable period follows where this blemish is fiddled with *ad nauseum*. When this behaviour is practised by waiters standing on the sidelines in restaurants, it is particularly off-putting.

Nail picking is another aspect of this behaviour and extends to cleaning out any detritus which has collected. This is then just flicked onto the floor, as would be the result of nose or ear mining.

Hawking up phlegm

This is a daily ritual for many, particularly the older Chinese. While walking in public parks in Hong Kong the hawks of passers-by can be offensive but they do not feel this is a private matter.

It is also something heard through the walls of apartment buildings when people hawk as a matter of course when brushing their teeth morning and night.

Spitting

There is a great deal less public spitting since the practice has been made a finable offence, but it does still occur. Sometimes it is the result of hawking but not always. It might be an attempt to get rid of a bitter taste or an antipathy to saliva in the mouth. In fact, anything which is felt to be "not right" in the mouth will be spat out, particularly by runners and walkers in public parks.

Shaking the legs on sitting

This is considered very unacceptable in Chinese society and children are constantly corrected on the habit. It consists of jiggling one or both legs the moment the person sits down.

Yun Yeeu Fook Bok, 人搖福薄, people shake less fortunate

Sew Yeeu Yeep Lok, 樹搖葉落, tree shake leaves fall – is an idiom used to remind people to stop shaking.

The decibel level

Many Cantonese speak very loudly indeed. They do not mean to shout at you but, generally for environmental reasons, have become accustomed to talking loudly to be heard and do not take into account the ambient noise levels.

If you ask people to "stop shouting" at you, this may occasionally offend, but more often it does the trick and the voice is moderated. Generally, the offender is not even aware the decibel level is out of the ordinary – let alone approaching the realm of eardrum-splitting pain.

Sye seng dee, 細聲啲, small sound more, is the Cantonese saying to request someone to lower the noise level. The request is accompanied by a hand gesture whereby you use your flat palm to imitate pushing something down. The hand gesture also indicates that you should calm down, all is not as bad as you seem to believe.

Removing shoes

In hot and humid weather, wearing leather shoes all day long can be uncomfortable. Sandals may not be appropriate work wear, so people take their shoes off when they sit down. They want to air their feet and do not give any thought to the fact that they may be dirty, or even smelly, and offend those in the vicinity.

This is one of the reasons you seldom see lace-up footwear on Cantonese. One noteworthy exception is the trend towards wearing sports shoes when not playing sports.

Athlete's foot is known as "Hong Kong foot", *Herng Gong gerk*, 香港腳, in Cantonese.

When British soldiers were first stationed in Hong Kong, army boots were part of the uniform. In the humid conditions, many suffered foot fungus and the British doctors, having no idea of the cause, called it "Hong Kong foot."

32

SHOWING RESPECT

Invitations

It is common practice to give invitation cards to a whole group but not expect all of them to attend. For example, you might invite all colleagues of similar standing to you to attend your wedding and expect them to know which invitations are "real" and which are just to give face. It is not proper to ask directly if an invitation should be taken as a real request that you attend the function, but you might ask others in the group if you should accept without offending or if the invitation was just issued to you to give you face.

Double talk

The watchmen (security guards) in residential buildings have built up a sort of double talk which is intended to show their friendliness towards you and that they recognise you and your frequent visitors.

A married man inviting a female friend home might be confronted with the watchman saying "A new girlfriend, Mr Smith?"

If you arrive home very late, he is likely to say, "You're home early tonight!"

When conservatively dressed and going out with your aunt and uncle, expect to hear, "Going to a party tonight?"

At the threshold

Traditional Chinese architecture includes a raised area at the threshold to both the building and the main gate to the compound. The step is often made of wood and generally between six and 18 inches high. Its purpose is as a barrier to flood and dust.

Over the years, it became taboo to place one's foot on this barrier. Additionally the high step meant that to negotiate the threshold it was necessary to look down at your feet. The combination of bowing one's head and taking a large step when entering a temple, hall, or the house of a decent man, is seen as a simple mark of respect.

Choosing given names

It is disrespectful to name your child after a living relative in the direct line; very different from the Western habit of offering respect to your grandfather by naming your son after him.

Traditionally, this stricture also applied to naming a child after the Emperor but this has relaxed. It offers no disrespect these days to call a child after a government leader. The prohibition only applies to Chinese names, not Western names.

How do, 孝道**, filial piety**

Chinese consider taking care of one's parents is a family responsibility and not something for the government. In China, it is an actionable matter to not take care of the financial burdens of your parents in old age.

Someone who does not take care of his parents is distrusted by the community at large.

Confucianism teaches:

*Lo mm lo, yee kup yun jee lo,*老吾老以及人之老

Yow mm yow, yee kup yun jee yow, 幼吾幼以及人之幼

Care for the elderly in your own family and then for those in other families,

Care for the young and helpless in your own family and then for those in other families.

As a result, the general care of the elderly and the less fortunate is highly developed in the Chinese community.

It is unthinkable that children would be excused from family activities such as ancestor worship, funerals, weddings, and reunion dinners. The behaviour of the various participants is closely ordered and certain forms of obeisance are owed to the differing degrees of relationship in the family unit.

Saving face

If they find they have been cheated, Chinese are more likely to accept what they see as their failure in not having realised that the product was counterfeit or the con artist was a criminal, than they are to report it. It is taken as a lesson in life and there is a grudging admiration for the perpetrator as it is considered clever to get around the grey areas of the law.

Production of products or foodstuffs which endanger human safety or life are another matter. This is not tolerated and a great outcry will ensue.

33

LIVE AND LET LIVE

Gay sor but yook, mut see yew yun, 己所不欲, 勿施於人, **live and let live**

This Confucian teaching is the equivalent of the English, do unto others as you would have them do unto you. The strict adherence to this principle may well be behind the extraordinarily low rate of crime against the person in Hong Kong. The low rate of vandalism, hooliganism, theft, etc., may also be down to this.

Personal safety on Hong Kong's streets

Newcomers to Hong Kong and tourists can often be recognised by the way in which they guard against casual theft and muggings.

There is an obvious police presence on the street in Hong Kong and crackdowns against Triad activity have been largely successful. In addition, the Cantonese have no history of violent crime against the person for monetary gain.

When Clare first came to Hong Kong, she had been living in Sydney where she had purchased a dog for safety as it was dangerous to walk on her own. It was many months before the constant low-level fear with which she had been living dissipated.

Now, when Clare travels out of Hong Kong, she finds herself being careless to the point that locals warn her of the risks she is taking. This experience is common to Hong Kongers when travelling.

Not only the streets, but public parks are also quite safe. Cantonese in summer often sleep on park benches and the police do not move them on. They sleep in the open not because they do not have homes to go to, it is simply a matter of enjoying the pleasant temperatures to the full.

Local women carry handbags gaping open, men carry bulky wallets in their back pockets, and backpacks and waist bags worn outside the clothes are common, without worrying about pickpockets. There are a few areas where pickpockets are active: on the Star Ferry, some busy streets, certain supermarkets. It is not all over Hong Kong, though, and most people are not vigilant.

Unattended personal belongings and deliveries are commonplace. At sporting venues, bags are just left indiscriminately and the owners expect to find them when they have finished playing. Outside restaurants, baskets of vegetables are left on the doorstep until staff arrive to open up.

Using public space

It is quite normal to see public areas being used for private business purposes. Magazines and newspapers routinely use footpaths as distribution centres.

Private individuals also make free with public areas. Winter quilts, for instance, are aired over the facilities in children's playgrounds or handrails along the street.

Making jokes at another's expense

Cantonese might be accustomed to shrugging off the ham-fisted efforts of foreigners to engender good feelings by making jokes, but a bad feeling always lingers.

Most Western jokes DO NOT TRANSLATE into Chinese and the sense of humour of the two cultures is vastly different.

Chinese are not amused by "jokes" which deal with personal appearance, social status, religion, employment, or wealth in any form. They are taken as insulting and there is nothing in the armoury of the average Cantonese which allows any social response apart from looking and feeling hurt.

Cantonese jokes are mainly centred on language and the different meanings of words which sound the same. They are hard enough to explain in the original language, let alone attempt to translate.

Accepting a compliment

Cantonese and Western cultures have different attitudes towards accepting compliments. The compliments themselves are also quite different.

A Cantonese will compliment you that you look better than you did last time, often leading the Westerner to wonder what it was about them that looked so awful before. No such comparison is intended.

Westerners are taught to accept compliments gracefully whereas Cantonese are taught to deny the compliment and exhibit humility in all situations.

Another school of thought deals with not challenging the Gods. A compliment should be denied as otherwise the Gods might conclude that you think you are better than them, or are just plain vain. Either way, it may bring bad luck down upon you. This particularly applies to complimenting the looks or cleverness of babies which is close to taboo.

Dead Western foreigner

Say Gwye Lo, 死鬼佬, Dead Ghost Man! Never said to one's face but only behind Westerners' backs when they are behaving in a manner seen as strange or offensive by the Cantonese. This extremely commonly heard expression might sound very derogatory (and it is meant to be) but in fact it is one of the things about living in Hong Kong as a non-Chinese that is most attractive.

Cantonese operate in their daily lives very much on a "live and let live" basis. Unlike in many Western countries, where complete strangers will interfere in the way that others choose to comport themselves in public, Cantonese purposefully avoid interfering with strangers who are a little different.

This extends to people who behave in an anti-social fashion. Displays of public drunkenness or overt affection, for instance, are generally ignored.

Staring at people who are markedly different in stature, those who are very tall, with dark black skin, or hugely obese, for instance, is common. Anyone or anything which is different from the norm is stared at with an almost child-like fascination due to lack of exposure – and used to be accorded to white-skinned people as well. Cantonese ask themselves questions such as "How will he get in the bus (he is so tall)?" and stare at the person to find the answer.

There is no thought that the staring might be intrusive or could make the object of fascination feel uncomfortable. In Cantonese terms, it is something they would ignore themselves so why would it bother anyone else? If challenged to stop staring it is unlikely that the objection will be understood. Telling someone to mind his own business will be found hurtful. If you can be seen, you are his business!

Good-looking men and women attract a lot of attention. Passers-by are seen to walk into lamp posts and rubbish bins, they are so busy staring at the object of their desire.

Scantily dressed women attract both attention and comment. Cantonese women are very modest in their dress and this, largely, is fuelled by the intrusive ogling of Cantonese men who consider it a game to see how much of an unknown woman's body they can see, by looking down the top of her dress, for instance. This behaviour is considered very rude if the woman is known to the ogler.

Afterword

We hope this book has answered some of your questions about Hong Kong. It is an easy city to live in with a diverse population who all rub along together well enough. Personal tax is amongst the lowest in the civilised world, the people are welcoming, and the climate is not harsh.

Now that you are armed with a few of the cultural taboos, and have some of the regional behaviour explained, we hope you can put aside any ill feelings which might have spoiled your enjoyment of this exciting and international city.

The language barrier is not insurmountable. Cantonese, Mandarin and English are the three official languages of the territory.

The level of English in Hong Kong is not particularly high but most people have some English and are willing to try to understand what you want. Few Cantonese speak Mandarin well and jokes abound on the Mainland about Hong Kong people being foreigners when it comes to the Mandarin language and their approach to life.

We have tried to give you a few useful phrases in this book but it is not intended as a language teaching tool. With luck you will be understood or, if the worst comes to the worst, offer some amusement as you try to get your tongue around the unaccustomed sounds.

Hong Kong is a friendly city with diversions to suit the most discerning visitor. There are art galleries and museums, amusement parks and theatres, cinemas and karaoke lounges. There are many sporting organisations, public swimming baths and beaches, walking trails from the easy to the difficult, and, of course, lots of shopping as Hong Kong is still a duty-free port.

Public services in Hong Kong are among the best in the world. Public transport is clean, cheap, and reliable, the hospital system keeps up with the latest in both Western and Traditional Chinese medicine, and in fact leads the world in some areas. Business flourishes as investors are offered the protection of a common law jurisdiction, a well trained police force, an active anti-corruption body, and, above all, the Cantonese are deeply interested in food so whatever you want to eat you can probably find it. All that is needed now is for you to get out there and enjoy it.

EXPLORE ASIA WITH BLACKSMITH BOOKS

From retailers around the world or from *www.blacksmithbooks.com*

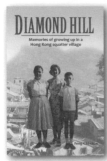

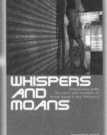